The Marketing Blueprint

Table of contents

Acknowledgments

I want this book to start by acknowledging the people who pushed me to make it possible. I want to thank my parents: Francois, Julie, Nathalie, and Richard, for giving me the chance to act on my dreams. It's not easy to raise someone with an entrepreneurial mindset like mine. I did not want to go to school, I did not want to get a job, and I was messy at times. I can understand why you felt I was a lost cause sometimes; I felt the same way occasionally. There is no pre-written plan for entrepreneurship; you simply have to do whatever you can to achieve your vision. I've progressed quite a bit throughout the years, and it's because of your help. You've given me the chance to show you what I could do and you've helped me the whole way. I hope you are proud of who I am, as you've instilled the fundamental pillars that I needed to become an effective entrepreneur. I still have a long way to go; however, I feel I take a new step every day. The journey is never ending, and I will take advantage of every second.

"Just because the road ahead is long, is no reason to slow down."
— Ralph S. Marston Jr.

I also want to thank people close to me that have helped make this book a reality. First off, I want to thank Patrick, for helping me edit this book. It's much harder to write an English book when your first language is French. I want to thank my friend Jimmy, for letting me come to his place and brainstorm on life and philosophy; those sessions helped me think deeper, and to look at marketing concepts as an art, not just a business. I couldn't have done it without my girlfriend, Florence, and my sister, Anaïs, for their advice. They helped me cope with the stress I experienced while writing this book. I may not have taken all their advice in stride, but I truly appreciate all the enthusiasm you had for my project. I want to thank every other person close (and not-so-close) to me that believed I could write a marketing book at 21 years old. Finally, I want to thank all my loyal followers across all mediums. Without your support, I would have never decided to write this book, and I would most certainly not be where I am today. Thanks to all of you, I love you all.

Even though these pages are meant to be the first you read, these are the last I'm writing. I wanted the start of this book to be introspective about the experience of writing a marketing book. It has been an insane ride; it changed my life. I learned more about myself and about marketing than I knew before, and I hope that evolution is reflected in the book. I've made new connections, I've made sacrifices to spend more time writing, I've received a lot of love from around the world, and I've received a lot of hate from people saying I was not able going to be able to accomplish it. But most of all, I've learnt about life and happily achieving, instead of achieving to be happy.

"The book that will most change your life is the book you write."
— Seth Godin

I did not write this book with the idea that I know everything. In fact, I barely know anything. We all do. The greatest marketers understand this and happily proclaim it. Of course, I know marketing; I learnt it through hard work. Any marketer needs a solid fundamental base; but, after that, it's all about trying, being creative, having a vision, and not being afraid to execute. The world of marketing is in constant flux; to stay on top, one has to learn new things every day. A diploma may get your foot in the door; 10 years in, however, your results are entirely dependent on your willingness to stay active.

I am not some rich person trying to convince you that I will make you rich through what I know. I myself am not a millionaire, yet. I did not sell my business to Apple or Microsoft for millions of dollars. I had the chance to use my experience in my various ventures to create a successful consulting business. My untraditional vision and concrete results with my clients allowed me to build on my initial success.

This book is a summation of what I've learned, from working with clients, going out to dinner with marketing mentors and entrepreneurs, conversations with CEOs and marketing managers from all over the world (such as Barnes & Nobles and Walmart), reading marketing books, working my way up, and going to seminars and conferences. Despite all these great sources, my greatest teacher has been my own life: dropping school to grow my brand, and going from nothing, to having impacted over 1000 businesses.

Some entrepreneurs wait until they are very far into their careers to share what they know and their story with the world. I've decided to take a different approach. Instead, I decided that I would take the world with me on this journey towards success. I am forever grateful that you've decided to join me on this path.

I've tried to make this book as simple as possible, and as complete as possible. You can read it from cover to cover if you choose, or you can read random chapters. This book is meant to teach, reteach, or otherwise hone your marketing skills. I chose to make this book as timeless as possible, so that it remains just as effective in the future as it does now. I handpicked the best advice I've given clients, and the greatest lessons I've ever been given.

Marketing books have one frequent flaw. They are too theory-centric, and designed for a classroom environment. The theories were excellent and well explained, but the books never gave practical situations to use them in. This is what made me decide to have this book be much more practical; rather than theoretical. Whether you are a CEO, marketing manager, or an entrepreneur starting out, this book will give you a fresh, young, and practical view on marketing. It will help you become a better marketer.

After knowing the core basics of marketing, I believe marketing is all about having ideas, executing them with intuition, smarter strategies, curiosity, boldness, and passion. It is much more than knowing fancy terms that come from a textbook. It's about accomplishing something... and having fun!

I hope this book reflects how strongly I feel about the art of marketing, and how much fun it can be to succeed in this amazing industry.

About Me

I was born in 1994. I may be young, but, as you will attest, that has never stopped me. Let me walk you through my life. I always had the instinct of an entrepreneur, even as a child. I had this urge to do and learn everything by myself. I taught myself violin at 5 years old. When I was 8, I wanted to become an actor. So, I took part of the most plays I could muster. My drive to succeed was always something I had. I may not be a famous actor, but I have consistently proved to myself that I can do anything I set my mind to.

At 10 years old, I started selling postal cards at my mother's hairdressing salon. Since then, I've never had what you'd call a "traditional" job. At 13 years old, I learned how to code by myself, and I coded my own search engine. I used my coding knowledge to start a small website for business development.

When I was 15, I decided to leave my hometown to play basketball in Michigan. I did not know anyone there, so I began emailing schools to know if they were looking for basketball players for their summer program. I was not a very proficient English speaker; I heavily relied on Google Translate to communicate. They accepted my request, and found a family where I could stay. I stayed there for 6 months, and learned English in the process.

When I was 16, I put all my money into recording equipment for audio and video. My goal was to become a recording artist. Two years later, I was touring the province, along with over 1 million views on my music videos. I also used my equipment to record other artists. As I was working on this new venture, an epiphany hit me: I'm an entrepreneur; this is what I want to do as a career. So, to make that happen, I began absorbing as much business and marketing content as I could.

While I was in the middle of my music business, I started a club promoting business. These events were where I first got to put my knowledge into real situations. Some of my parties were generating 3 000$ a night.

Yes, all these various ventures came at a price: I had to leave school to properly pursue them. I believe, however, that I am just as knowledgeable, if not more, than any Ivy League graduate. I taught myself with books used in university, and I have had the most powerful teacher of them all: experience.

One day, I had a realization. If I am successful marketing my own projects, why not earn my living helping other people achieve theirs? I started with one client, and saw my list grow more every day. I learned marketing the hard way. But, I don't know everything. If a marketer tells you he knows everything about marketing, do not hire him. Marketing constantly changes; no one can ever know all about it.

I have seen clients increase their revenue by 400% in the two months I worked with them. I've had the chance to see companies grow from 40 000$ to 3 million $ in annual revenue. In other words, I have helped my clients see as much success as they could. I have worked with some of Canada's top brands, and recently took my platform to the international stage, thanks to the Internet.

I am believer in the idea of generating a following online. With the large audience I had gained, I could become an endorser of various projects. One of my notable investments include an iPhone game with a 1000$ advertising budget. It currently has 300 000 on the App Store. That's huge, and I am proud of it. If ever the game interests you, go ahead and look up "Squid Up" on the App Store.

In 2012, I invested in a small clothing brand called Wuup Clothing. I saw its potential, and I jumped right in. One year into my initial investment, the brand has climbed 2400% in monthly revenue. Last year, I sold my shares last year to focus on my consulting business and other future projects. My one year with Wuup taught me quite a bit on managing start-ups.

I am currently dividing my time working on writing, consulting, creating marketing information products, and building my personal brand. I also have several side projects, as well as small time investing on the stock market. When I am not working, I try to travel, to read, to experience new things, to eat good food, and to enjoy life as much as possible.

Don't be shy; follow my journey on Instagram (@julesmarcoux), on Facebook, and on my website (www.julesmarcoux.com) to learn more about my new projects and products. I often offer free products for anyone willing to give me their ear.

Cheers, to life!

The "Coolness Points" Strategy

Experts keep talking about word-of-mouth and how it is crucial to your business. They keep saying that you need to have people talk about you if you want to succeed. But they never really talk about how you can generate word-of-mouth.

Bottom line is, word-of-mouth is the ONLY way to not be tied to your advertising budget. That's one of the biggest points of marketing. Let me explain:

Without word-of-mouth (these numbers are hypothetical, based on my experience):
- You invest 10 000$ purely for advertising.
- 600 000 people see your ad.
- 25% are really interested (150 000).
- In this 150 000, only 50% are willing to pay (75 000).
- In this 75 000, only 10% will take the time to either call you, or make any inquiries about buying (7 500).

- In this 7 500, you will close only 10% (750).
- Let's say your product earns 115$ in revenue per unit. That's 86 250$.
- Therefore, you invested 10 000$ in advertising and it generated 86 250$ of revenue.

Now, in a vacuum, these would be solid results. However, when accounting for business expenses and costs related to the creation and distribution of your product, these same results don't look so great. On top of that, since there is no word-of-mouth occurring, you will need to RE-INVEST 10 000$ to RE-GENERATE 86 250$ of revenue. Also, keep in mind that the longer your ads are out there, the less people will pay attention to them. The goal is not to earn more money by investing more money. The goal is to create more "Brand-Advocates" (That's what we call people that talk about your brand or product to their friends).

Another important point of marketing (especially advertising) is to create a brand that can go on "autopilot". In other words, it sells itself. Let's tie this back to the previous example: if you would have integrated word-of-mouth into your campaign, the initial $86 250 could have turned into $258 750 if every buyer would have brought you 3 of their friends. That's a small example. Look at Walt Disney or Starbucks. They depend on having Brand Advocates to rake in new customers.

The trick is, you have to get people to WANT to tell a friend about your brand.

There is a quote that I like. I unfortunately do not know the author's name: "Money doesn't talk anymore. People do. That's why you need to rethink your marketing strategy."

So right now at this moment, ask yourself: "Would anyone go out of their way to tell a friend about me?"

Regardless of what you are marketing, be it a service or product, you have to ask yourself this essential question.

If your answer is yes, then ask yourself: "are you sure? Why would they go out of their way for that?" Take time to reflect on that. Then, ask yourself this final question: "how can I MAKE SURE they'll go out of their way?" There are plenty of strategies that can generate word-of-mouth; but I tend to lean towards a specific strategy. I've taken to calling it "Coolness Points."

Make it so that people earn "Coolness points" by talking about you.

UNIQLO, a Japanese clothing retailer, does pop-up shop events in different cities every year. For each individual event, they tell exclusively where this popup shop will be located to a bunch of lucky fans. They are the first to know, and because they are the first, they will talk about it. The distinction of being first makes them talk about it.

There is a restaurant in New York called "Please Don't Tell". All they have is a very simple website, with no information at all, except for a phone number. Plus, they never advertise. To enter the restaurant, you need to enter a phone booth, pick up the telephone, and then tell your name. It feels like a secret, and people WILL talk about a secret. People want to give others the impression they know something others don't. It gives "Coolness Points". Make information "exclusive", and people will talk about it.

Here are some examples that come to my mind; this could help you develop your own "Coolness Points" tactic:

So, if you have a restaurant, why not try a secret menu? Starbucks did it, and it grew their sales.

If you're marketing a hot sauce, you could write a fictional agreement stating that customers won't sue because it's too spicy. They will brag about how they consumed the hottest sauce ever.

If you own a hair-salon, you could introduce a secret card that gives customers a free glass of wine when they visit you.

If you own an online clothing store, why not give bonuses to customers for successful referrals, and added incentives to become a member?

If you work in the music industry, member benefits are also a possibility, offering exclusive songs and merchandise to the most dedicated fans.

Another idea would be to use influential people to your advantage. If you market watches, sending exclusive watches to influential people would make them talk about your brand very positively due to the treatment they are getting.

Using people's need for status is another way to generate word-of-mouth. For example, having a reward card with varying levels at a hotel (bronze, silver, gold, etc.) would make customers stay repeatedly, and definitely talk to all their social circle about their newest status at this hotel. People enjoy having high status, why not taking advantage of it?

Therefore, whatever type of business you are, or whatever you need to sell, make your customers see that earning "Coolness Points" and talking about your brand are synonymous. Give them the chance to brag a little bit. They will love this, and you will gain a larger clientele. A great, inexpensive method to boost profits.

"It's art when your **insurance** broker says, 'You know, there's a guy down the street who can sell you something better than I can.' "
— Seth Godin

Marketing can only be truly malicious when it sells malicious products. This is the golden rule that I abide to. It directs my entire approach to marketing. I've realized that, for marketing to be truly effective, it can't emphasize selling, but human interaction instead: helping people, reassembling people, and contributing to a better world.

I try to call my family more often. I try to go out with my friends more often. I try to lunch with new people more often, regardless of if I have an ulterior motive or not. I just want to become the best human being I can be, to share love around me and to help the most people I can.

Honesty and love are the best investments in business and life.

I have so much confidence in myself, and what I sell. Forcing a sale on someone, who has no need for my product, would be a disservice to him, myself, and society.

Chances are, it wouldn't work for him; that would harm both of us.

How to Rock a Sales Meeting & Business Development Meeting

I often hear that marketing and sales are different aspects of business. On paper, definitely. I, however, believe they belong together, in what I'd call the "growth department". Yes, marketing creates leads and sales close them. And that's the key: successful businesses recognize that these two concepts come together, not apart.

That being said, with the venue of the internet, growing a business has never been easier. But sometimes, we forget the power of meetings and business development done face-to-face. It is more important than ever to create deals, partnerships and human relations. This train of thought pushed me to write a chapter about some points I deem cannot be ignored when heading to a sales meeting.

The incredible business plan that will be essential to starting your business will come in due time. It is essential, however, that you know how to act when in a meeting to ensure this ideal plan gains the audience it needs.

Without further ado, here's my favourite checklist for a great sales meeting:

Dress for the sale

It true: dressing for the sale can have a powerful impact on the way you sell. Dressing nicely improves your own confidence, and also impacts the way your prospect and client sees you. Even if you are having the meeting over the phone, make sure you are dressed neat. This will improve your confidence and dramatically improve your chances to close the sale.

Find something of mutual interest and start with it

First of all, there are two things you need to avoid talking about: Politics and Religion. That being said, always make sure you start with something of mutual interest that will incite your prospect to talk about himself. Everybody loves to talk about themselves, and that will help your potential client to have confidence in you appreciate you. Never start with something too direct, like talking about the product you are selling, or something too soft and insignificant, like talking about the weather.

Know your objectives heading into the meeting

I've seen many clients and entrepreneurs come to me saying they need to get more leads. I then answer that with a question: are you closing the leads you have? Do you know exactly what to do when you have a lead in front of you? So much entrepreneurs have a lot of success getting in front of people, but they don't know how to close once they're in front of them. Make sure you know the goal of the sales meeting before you get there. Is it to set up a demo for your product? Is it to better understand the needs of your client to write a powerful and concrete proposal tailored for those needs? Is it to close a sale? If yes, know the exact sale you plan on closing. Your goal needs to be clear. Crystal clear.

Make sure to follow up

A survey conducted by the National Sales Executive Association reveals that only 10% of sales professionals are following up with leads more than three times. And, did you know that 90% of the sales are made over the 5th contact with your leads? In fact, according to this survey, 90% of the sales are made by only 10% of the sales people. So let's keep it simple and clear: if you want to become one of the best closers and marketers around, make sure you follow up with your leads. Even if there is no interest at the first meeting. A great follow up is normally around 48 hours after the proposal has been read, or that you offered something clear to your prospect. You have to keep the momentum going.

Look into their eyes

Eye contact is a very important aspect of a sale. When you state your price, make sure you look the person in the eyes and say what you want to say with confidence. The worst thing you can do is avoiding eye contact when closing a sale.

Be prepared, do your research, and get there early

Make sure you are early at a sales meeting. I always try to get there at least 20 minutes before, and I find the closest coffee shop around the meeting to work a little bit before the meeting. There is nothing more important than being ready. There is nothing worse than being late. Top closers are always the first in the room. To help you getting prepared, I have built a simple checklist that you can check before going into a sales meeting.

☐ Am I dressed for the sale?
☐ I have found something of mutual interest: _____ and I will start the conversation with it.
☐ I know the goal of the meeting. I want to _____
☐ I am there at least 20 minutes before. The closest coffee shop of the meeting is _____

☐ I have done my research about the prospect and gathered all the important information that will help me close the sale.

☐ I have followed-up (This is for after the meeting, after 48 hours or so have passed)

The Best Growth Strategy?
Using Your Phone

This strategy is one of the most subtle, and effective, business development/sales strategies. Its power lies in its simplicity. Entrepreneurs often ask me to develop a crazy sales strategy; when often, calling potential clients is as good, if not better. Despite the massive amount of social media, and methods of communication, I believe one of the best methods to grow your brand is calling on your phone.

If you went and called 10 people, offering your product to them, chances are that by the end of the week, you will make a sale. People like spending on themselves, and having a chance to help a starting brand while earning something on their end is a definite motivator.

I believe that the biggest reason why marketers and entrepreneurs fail is due to the fact that they do not ask to sell. Not that their product is inferior, or that they lack sales skills. That they simply don't ask.

I have clients and friends who have grown their businesses without any sort of social media or advertising. They just called potential clients.

Here are some key questions marketers and salespeople should ask themselves:

- Are you picking up the phone enough and finding new prospects? Are you picking up the phone at all?
- Are you sending enough prospective emails to gather new business and sales opportunities?
- Are you reaching out to every single lead you've gotten?
- Once you're in contact with a prospect, are you selling, or simply talking?
- Are you clearly asking for the sale when one-on-one with the customer?

These are key questions that should be considered. If any of the answers are no, then you know what to improve. Selling problems tend to be addressed by these questions.

Studies have found that the best way to propose a sale is to ask questions that cannot be answered by a yes or a no. This can be employed at any point in the sale: from initial contact with a client, to closing the sale at the end. Psychologically, the goal is to never have a prospect to say "no". For example, instead of asking "Are you interested in trying our product?" ask, "Which day would be best for us to give you a demo of our product?" When closing a retail sale, for example, instead of asking "Do you want to proceed to the cash register?" instead ask, "Will you be paying by cash or credit?"

I used sales as an example, but this strategy is applicable to anything that requires persuasion. Therefore, in any area of negotiating, which is a large part of business, avoiding yes/no answers is very effective. I have personally seen changes in my sales closing abilities because of it. There are other ways that this strategy can be used, apart from directly phoning clients. For example, if you are an online clothing brand owner, it's evident that you won't be calling potential buyers on their personal phone. Instead, use this exercise to call prospective wholesalers, distributors, boutiques that would be interested in buying in bulk, and even journalists. They could serve as good publicity.

Go ahead and prepare a list of prospects you want something from, and, beside their name and info, indicate exactly what you want from them. It could be for anything: to buy your product, to give you a contact you need, to distribute your product in their network, or for anything else related to business development. Evaluate how much you attempt to make contact with new prospects, and increase that number by 25%.

Sometimes the best way to obtain something is to ask for it. If you want more, ask more! Pick up the phone more and write more emails, you will be surprised with the results.

When I began building my social media following, I had no clear purpose for it. I just had this conviction that, in order to succeed, I had to build an audience. With this audience behind me, I could succeed.

This motivated me to create my own personal brand, and its audience started to grow. At the time, I was not selling a product; merely consulting for clients. I just kept sharing ideas and stories, hoping that it would eventually bring me that large following I coveted. I wanted to inspire regular people to do something with their life, no matter their motivation.

At the time of publication, I currently have 100 000 followers across all platforms. I am not saying this to brag; rather, I am proud that some random French Canadian can manage to make a big enough impact on the world, and share my knowledge with society. Hopefully, I can inspire others to do the same.

The reward of our work is not what we get, but what we become.
— Paulo Coelho

Build an Audience

With today's evolving technology, it has become more possible than ever to build, and retain, an audience. Your ability to build your brand depends on how well you can cater to an audience.

Many "Hollywood" type people have large followings (celebrities, athletes, models, etc.); however, I believe making an audience for a brand is just as possible to accomplish. Great marketers do not look only for customers, but for fans.

I've always invested in my own audience, and this gives me a kick-start every time I launch a new project or product, as I already have people aware of my new offerings. This advice doesn't only apply to personal brands. I believe having a strong audience can give any brand an edge over its competitors. It directs sales where you want them to go, and it creates many brand advocates. These people can be very powerful at making or breaking your company. People listen to other people; hearing good things from people unassociated with the company is always a good thing.

Audiences allow you to have a shortcut whenever releasing a new product. You will gain an immediate sales base. Also, advertising becomes simpler, as your target market is already awaiting your next offering.

Every audience needs to be nurtured, and treated like they're special. Make sure you share stories, content, and free stuff with them. Keep the rewards going, and establish a momentum that consistently makes them feel grateful to be a client of your brand. Sharing with your clients not only helps them retain interest, but also gives you the opportunity to spread your brand's image and message in different mediums.

Here are some tips to building a loyal fan base:

- Build your email list. Give something away in exchange for their email, ask for their email at the cash register, and/or put an opt-in widget on your website to incite people to subscribe.
- Grow your social media accounts. Network with other like-minded groups to exchange content promotion, create a giveaway, and interact with more people.

Give yourself a target growth number you want to achieve every week.

- Organize events to celebrate milestones. It can be effective to interact with your audience in person just as much as online.
- Attend more tradeshows. Always seek to get their emails so you can reach them.
- Make sure you constantly update your address list. Your audience is not only clients; business development contacts must feel important too.
- Social media advertising is a powerful tool; I suggest anyone looking to build an audience to look into it.

There are tons of ways to gain an audience and have it grow. Experiment to see what fits your brand best.

One key point I want to mention here: B2B brands should never shy away from building a fan base. I've seen so many entrepreneurs tell themselves that they don't need to create an audience, an email list, or their social media accounts, because they sell to businesses. Remember: your B2B decision maker is a regular customer after 5PM. Also, it has been proven that businesses are more willing to hire a business that their customers love. So, building your brand and building an audience with the public, even if you sell to businesses, is just as efficient.

Take advantage of the fact that crafting an audience is easier now than it used to be.

Building an audience will help you rely less on advertising to produce results, as you will already be talking directly to your customers. Give yourself specific goals to attain every week, and reach those goals efficiently to really take advantage of the benefits of having fans.

Create your cult following, and they'll create your success.

Build a Pre-Buzz

Imagine opening the doors to your store on opening day. You expect to see people running in, pushing each other like it's a Target on Black Friday. Unfortunately, this will never happen, unless you build awareness about your brand, and make them want to run in.

Many entrepreneurs and marketers get this backwards. They spend so much money, time, resources, and energy building a great product and distribution channel, that they forget one of the most crucial points to success: creating demand. One of the most fatal errors an entrepreneur can make is creating demand after the product is released. They may have a great product, but no client is interested. The expenses start coming in. Now, they've made a new worst enemy: time. They're doing whatever they can to build awareness, without any real, fundamental base to build off of.

The solution to their problem would have been to create pre-buzz. In other words, have clients before having the product. This strategy works not only in starting companies, but for any "new" situation: launching a new project, product, entering a new industry, and reaching a new segment of the market.

For example, an American brand trying to expand to China would be wise to build awareness a couple of months before the product is distributed. The company could even start building awareness before having distributors, giving them bigger negotiation power, and a higher chance to land better distributors due to higher demand.

The distribution strategy should be planned in unison with the demand's growth. Think about it this way: the demand leads the rest. Focusing on demand as your indicator of business will generate more buzz and sales momentum. The distribution strategy will be built, step-by-step, as the demand is established. Ask yourself: can the demand sustain the distribution? A good strategy would be to sell online, and with a few select retailers; once the demand increases, start looking at broader options.

There are many ways you can build awareness and increase demand. From PR, to advertising, to using people with high social influence, there are no bad methods to get the population to talk about you. By increasing awareness, you have a higher chance of the distributors already knowing about your product. Thus, you will be able to negotiate better with them, since they recognize the business opportunity. You will be in position of power.

Once brand awareness has reached a level you are comfortable with, now is the time to create the distribution network you will need, through networking, calling, and business development.

This concept was effectively used by Ciroc, when trying to enter the Quebec alcoholic beverage market. The Vodka brand, owned by Diageo, was trying to get through the door of the SAQ (governmental institution that controls liquor). Even though this process is much harder to accomplish than in most areas, they were not deterred. Instead, they decided to market private events in restaurants across the province, so people could try Ciroc before it had a market presence in the province. When they finally got into the SAQ, sales skyrocketed.

Redbull actually placed empty cans in various public spaces to create the impression that it was a popular beverage. This was done before Redbull established a strong distribution strategy. That is an incredibly clever way to create demand for an unknown product.

In conclusion, always have customers lined up before distributing a product. Whether it is for a new company, or for an existing product reaching new markets. Then, establish a distribution strategy that grows based on the demand that is being created.

"Life is like riding a bicycle. To keep your balance, you must keep moving."
— Albert Einstein

When you're afraid of going forward, you fall. By advancing, you constantly prevent the worst thing that could happen: falling. You might fail, but look at it this way. A cyclist and someone, who is terrified of biking, have an accident. The cyclist will know why he fell, and will make sure it doesn't happen again; he will continue biking, however. The other person will make sure it doesn't happen by never biking again. I had an acquaintance tell me something that still sticks with me now: doubt will get you out of action, and action will get you out of doubts.

Success is waiting for you. Stop overthinking it, and move forward like it's the Tour de France.

You won't be doubting yourself again.

Keep the momentum

Let's get it straight: marketing is all about momentum. The day you stop building your brand is the day it will start to perish. A lot of people think a business can "stay" where it is. They think that, if they reach a certain milestone, they can then stop and stay there. Unfortunately, in just about everything, nothing stands still; it is either progressing or regressing.

I'll use a metaphor to make this idea easier to grasp. Use this image as a description of the world; more specifically the business side of it.

See the marketplace as a big hill you are climbing, and see your brand as a big, heavy wheel you are trying to push toward this hill. If you keep pushing, it will gain momentum, and the wheel will keep rolling, making the process easier. The only thing is that, if you stop pushing, it will slow down, and eventually roll over you and get back to the foot of the hill.

We could also picture this concept as riding a wave. Once you start riding the wave, you can't stop. The fun part about marketing is that the hill has no top, and the wave has no end.

Have a look at the first mega-brands, such as Bakers (Since 1765), Colgate (1806), Jim Bean Bourbon (1795), Tiffany & Co (1837), Mott's (1842), American Express (1850), Jell-O (1897), John Deer (1837), and Coca-Cola (1886).

What do they all have in common? They've kept their momentum going with their brand since the beginning.

There are tons of examples that prove that brands can last, as long as they have their feet on the gas pedal. After all, isn't the goal of marketing to ensure business longevity?
The fact that these brands have lasted this long is no accident. Yes, there are some uncontrollable external factors, but they pale in comparison to what marketers can control. Here are some key concepts that helped them achieve long-term excellence.

They see marketing their brand as a marathon, not a sprint

When you play the marketing game, you're playing for the long term. If you stop investing in your brand, your customers will go to the competition. The human brain forms habits, so expect your customers to do the same. Don't expect your brand to succeed exclusively off of a 100 000$, two week advertising campaign. You won't win an award for customer service by smiling a ton for two weeks.

One thing you must always ask yourself: Can my brand, and I, sustain what we're doing long term?

For example, don't invest 100 000$ in advertising for two weeks, unless you expect to be doing it regularly. Instead, you could invest 100$ a day, and stick to that strategy for a long time. If you're comfortable with just 1$ a day, that's fine; As long as you keep the momentum at the same rate. As profits rise, so can your budget. But make sure your actions remain constant.

This will establish a strong culture within the business, and send a consistent message to consumers. Take carmakers for example. If you praise yourselves as the safest cars on the market, stick with that. Don't start touting your speed; your clients aren't there for that, and new consumers will look elsewhere. Your long-term message should not see much change.

This doesn't only apply to advertising. Every aspect of marketing must hold the same, consistent message. If red is a main color of your company, use it in everything; don't suddenly swipe it for lime-green. If you give free samples, do not suddenly stop.

By being constant, you will see your message become ingrained in customers' heads.

Marketing is a never-ending race. To stay first, make sure you're constant. There will always be new markets to conquer, new techniques to develop, new products to build, and new ideas to execute. Make it your mission to stay active as a brand.

They stay young

Long-term brands, no matter how old, always find ways to stay "trendy." If brand failure is a marketer's greatest fear, being a "one hit wonder" is the second greatest. We want to be able to have our brand stay successful. That is achieved through constant repositioning, and never settling with the now.

Great brands recognize when their target market loses interest. When this happens, they reposition themselves to gain back attention and loyalty. Great brands understand that, if they stop innovating, their product will lose power and attraction. This is why they keep coming up with new ideas, and follow new market trends; regardless of whether it's for marketing strategies, or for their core product.

Great brands look to reinvent themselves every day. It is how they stay relevant.

As you might have noticed, all these points have something in common: momentum. Brands that last, are brands that move.

Of course, other elements have contributed to brands' longevities. However, all of them follow these three main pillars of momentum, which puts every chance on their side for consistent success.

Therefore, think about the hill. To push your wheel, you can never relent. You need to learn to conserve your energy, so that the wheel can always move up. Burning yourself out in a minute will bring you back to the bottom.

If you aspire to become a legendary brand, never settle. As you take a break from going up the hill, others will take your place. Learn it from the pros: momentum is key for continued success.

Get the Name Right

Developing an effective brand name is an essential aspect of marketing your brand. It is the thing that people will use to talk about you; it will be there from your brand's inception to its end. It will define the personality of your brand. People might say a brand is just a name. On the contrary: would Coca-Cola still be Coca-Cola if they changed their name, while retaining an identical product? No! The same goes for well branded companies such as Apple, Kleenex, or Canon.

Generic words are deadly

Giving a generic name to your brand is the worst thing you can do. It was working in the early nineties. However, the early nineties have passed. Here are a few examples of generic brand names: The Hotel Company, Hotels.com,

BookStores Quebec, Quality Clothings Co., Books.com, Shop.ca.

In 1997, McAfee, a leading internet security brand, bought Network Associates, another leading internet security brand. They decided to stick with the brand name "Network Associates". They invested more than 10 million$ into their brand new advertising campaign, including a 30 second spot at the Super Bowl. It failed miserably. People were listening to the ads and wondering what the brand's purpose was! It is so generic, that it was passing through the heads of consumers without making any sort of lasting impression. McAfee reverted to their original name a few years later, to no one's surprise.

The same thing happened to eToys.com. They invested large amounts of money to get their name into the heads of consumers, without any results. The name was too generic.

People are busy and don't have time to consciously learn about your brand, so develop a brand name that sticks; not a generic word. You'll spend much less time trying to create a lasting image.

Make it significant

Since your brand name will be the most mentioned words when talking about your company, make sure that your brand name is remarkable, while also making your brand significant.

I can hear the naysayers already: how can I accomplish them without a generic brand name? Here's the answer: with personality. In fact, up to 60% of the top global brands are completely made up words, with a touch of eccentricity. For example: Nike, Rolex, Adidas, Visa, Sprite, Kleenex or even Nokia. It is with years of marketing efforts that those brand succeeded at making their made-up words significant. They didn't TAKE a word that is already significant, they MADE theirs significant. Of course, those brands came up with those names by mixing words or by making them up completely.

So, my best advice when coming up with a brand name, is to ask your community if your brand name fits your brand's personality. That's why it is essential to know your brand's values and target market. Would you call a new baby clothing brand "Alders," even if it's made up? No, because that sounds like "Elders" which would be more suitable for older people. If you are creating a comedy events company, try to find a name that sounds funny, without being generic. Try to find something catchy, young and memorable. Just For Laughs is an example. Something that has a musical sound, or rolls off the tongue, is also an effective method of naming your brand. So, go ahead: brainstorm different names and try to come up with 6 to 7 different names. Always keep in mind the personality of your brand, work with sounds related to that personality.

Keep it short

Notice the pattern of the names I cited in the last section: Nike, Rolex, Adidas, Visa, Sprite, Kleenex, and Nokia. The longest name in that list is 7 letters. When I work with clients to find new brand names, I always try to see if we can shrink the names we came up with. A great example of how a generic brand became a good brand by shrinking it is Intel. Instead of calling the brand Intelligent, they shrank it and called it "Intel". As we keep saying, good brands are catchy and easy to remember. That's why I always advise clients to keep their brand names short; not more than 3 or (maybe) 4 syllables. Short names stay in the consumer's mind.

Do your research, and make sure you have a great domain name

As we live in the web era, it is important to do your research. When you've come up with a couple of potential brand names, make sure that you conduct your research to make sure that:

- There are other brand names with the exact brand name or close to it. Or, brands that sound exactly like your name.
- It has no negative connotation, in English or any other language (THIS IS IMPERATIVE).

- You can have at least several domain names with this name.

Brand naming is a fun process. Be creative, and remember: The best way to have a great idea, is to have a lot of ideas. Use all the imagination you have to find the next brand that everyone will instantly recognize.

"Courage is not the absence of fear, but rather the judgement that something else is more important than fear.
— Ambrose Redmoon

I had a thing for being afraid. Afraid of failure, afraid of heights, afraid of loving, afraid of starting something new, afraid of going somewhere, afraid to meet new people; the list goes on. I am still plagued by these fears occasionally; however, I have learned to combat them.

I was terrified when I initially launched myself into the business world. I still have moments of doubt. In these moments, I realize that my future, and my present achievements, give me no reason to doubt myself.

When I want to act, I simply hold my breath, and dive out of my comfort zone. I sometimes come back with treasure; I sometimes come back with a worn-out old boot. But, each time, it becomes easier to hold my breath and dive back in.

Don't be afraid of the water. Who knows what lies underneath it.

The Proper Way to Diversify

Product diversity is integral to a business' success. We all understand that business is about solving the customer's needs. By offering multiple products, you improve your sales, since you solve multiple needs. Here are some key techniques and concepts to develop your multi product strategy.

The first idea would be to offer different products that solve different needs. For example, a law firm could begin offering a specialized service for one of the problems their clients experience the most. Tech companies frequently diversify, due to the various needs of customers. Apple, for example, has the iPhone, iPod, and the iMac; all designed for various needs. Software service companies could sell tutorials on how to optimize business software within a business. This is the first step to adopting a diversified product strategy. Evaluate your market needs, and take advantage of what you aren't currently offering, but could feasibly do without radically changing your services. Ideally, your products should also promote each other for better effect. Apple's Apple TV can be used in unison with other Apple devices, promoting buying multiple products.

One of my favourite ways to diversify is by offering a wide price range for services. Subscription services are a business model that utilizes various prices effectively. For example, I offer a monthly gift service. Every month, I send a gift box to my customers. One box is worth 20$ alone. However, if customers buy multiple month packages, I would offer them with boxes costing 18$ each. That way, depending on what they're willing to pay, there is an option for them.

Service providers benefit from multiple products by offering premium and basic services. This way, they gain negotiating power, as they do not rely on a single source of income.

Both price and product diversification should be used; using them in unison yields the ideal result.

Let's take the Harvard brand, for instance. As a lot of people cannot attend it, they offer multiple solutions to make the brand more accessible. For example, they offer books, certificates, conferences, seminars, online articles, and more.

Their products not only solve different needs, but also come with different prices.

As the famous investor Warren Buffet once said: "Never depend on single income." By integrating multiple products to your brand strategy, you not only reduce your risk, but your customer base increases. This will help spur innovation as well. It will also deter you from discounting products, or losing negotiating power, as previously mentioned.

One thing to note: before diversifying, always make sure you have the time, money, and resources to add this new product/service. Introducing a product too early in your brand's strategy can cause your initial product to suffer, due to less resources being attributed to your essential, most important product. Your first "second" product is always best introduced when it is easy to scale, and is a complementary product to your first offering.

Make sure everything added to your brand is synonymous with your message, and only serves to strengthen your hold on your market niche. Becoming a Jack-of-all-trades is not ideal, as focusing on something always yields better results. Diversify your offerings, but stay focused on your niche.

Bic is a good example of lack of focus. Their office products were successful, so they decided to branch out. They ended up selling underwear. The product failed, because it had no link to what Bic is known for. Products should aim at attracting more customers, and reinforcing the image you want to uphold.

Broadening product lines can be a daunting task; however, successful diversity breeds success. Remember that, for it to be successful, synchronisation between every product should be strived for. They are all cogs in the machine that is your brand, not completely separate machines.

Think about how you can respond to more needs, while remaining the same company you were beforehand.

It's time for a little brainstorming.

A Brand is only as Strong as its Weakest Touch Point

"A chain is only as strong as its weakest link"
— Unknown

As a marketer, it is your duty to look at your brand from a third person perspective. You have to make sure all touch points are perfect. By definition, your brand's touch points are all the various ways a customer can interact with your brand directly. This is when customers will form a strong opinion on your brand. These touch points will determine if your customer becomes addicted to your brand, or avoids it at all costs.

Here is a list of sample touch points:

- Your advertisements
- How your employees answer the telephone (voicemail is included)

- Social Media (its appearance, and the attitude of the community on your page)
- Trade Shows (how you stand out from all the other kiosks)
- Networking (how you shake hands, your business card, your business pitch)
- Blogs (ones you own and collaborate on)
- Word of Mouth (what people say about you when you're around AND not around)
- Direct Mail & Newsletters
- Public Relations
- Websites (All the websites affiliated to your brand)
- Your logo and visual identity
- Packaging & Point of sales
- Emails (Business development emails, signatures, the way you write, grammar, etc.)
- Proposals that you send to potential and active customers
- The invoices you send to customers after a sale
- Speeches
- Your sponsors
- Employees
- Products

- Billboards
- Vehicles design
- Everything else that your customers are in touch with before, during, and after the sale

Every time your customer is in contact with your company, they are at a touch point. Every single one matters as much as the others.

This chapter is not about how to optimize one touch point in particular; I believe it's the marketer's job to optimize each touch point the brand possesses. This chapter is about how to properly evaluate your brand, from the right perspective. When evaluating for areas to correct, bias needs to be avoided. Using the right perspective makes optimizing touch points an easier, and more effective, process. Here are some tips for having a neutral point of view, along with effective optimization.

List all your touch points

The first step is to make a list of all the touch points your brand uses. There are many; strive for the biggest list possible. Of course, it may be hard to find a large number if it is the first time you evaluate touch points. However, do not stop until you've found a quantity that appears large to everyone, especially you.

I suggest using computer programs for this, such as Excel, in order to be able to save and modify the list at your leisure.

Evaluate and rate

Now the next step is to evaluate and rate every single touch point you listed. Don't review them yourself; have people unaffiliated with your company do the evaluations. The goal is to have a neutral perspective. Bias in the evaluations would lead to inaccurate portrayals of the population.

Then, give yourself a universal rating system, so that each touch point is evaluated the same way. Examples include from 1-10, Excellent to Needs Immediate Attention, and so on.

If you feel you have a network of contacts that could perform the evaluations for you, do not hesitate to ask for their services. However, ensure the surveys are anonymous; the anonymity usually provides honest results. Scientists typically run the same test over and over again to ensure they're correct. Don't be afraid to do the same with touch point evaluations.

Take action

The last step is to take corrective action, based off of your results. Start from the weakest points, and correct them as soon as possible.

Find at least one action that will ensure the touch point improves.

I always encourage my clients to perform an evaluation every two months. This way, quality is kept at a constant rate, and improved when needed. Since every touch point is equally important, not paying attention to one can be deadly. I always like to say: "A good logo won't compensate for a bad product, and a good product won't compensate for a bad logo." In other words, all touch points need to be synchronized in terms of quality. Make sure you constantly ensure this remains a standard.

Do your homework: every client needs to be satisfied with all touch points. It can only be good for your brand.

Give the Spotlight to your People

A great brand is all about its people. From the CEO, to the marketing manager, to the sales people; a great brand understands that its people are its greatest asset. This being said, the best marketers always seek to improve the personal branding of their teams.

There's a simple reason for this: the better your organization's team is, the better your brand is. More and more, customers love to do business with people, not just with corporations; it gives them a sense of forming a human relationship. Having a great personal brand also helps to improve your credibility in the eyes of your business contacts. This could help your employees close more deals, and attract better business opportunities, therefore giving you an advantage over the competition. The feeling of having a personal relationship with workers also motivates customers to stay loyal.

As is constantly iterated throughout these chapters, your people strategy must be synonymous to your brand image. The best way is to see the personal brand of your people as an extension of your business. If your company is called Pineapple Music, for example, make sure that the personal brand you are creating is not just John, but "John from Pineapple Music". The next few paragraphs will detail how to synchronize personal branding, with the entire brand of the organization.

In other words, giving your employees a brand of their own allows them to bring more value to your organization as a whole. It allows them to have a more "human" feel, to promote better, and to communicate to clients that your organization only hires the best talent.

Two of my favourite examples of successful personal branding across the entire organisation are with Google and the Virgin Group. Whatever your role is in the organisation, these two brands make sure that you have the right personal branding, and they give you the tools to develop it, making it very beneficial for the organization. Also, every personal brand works to promote the company, and the company works to improve the brand of its people, creating a long lasting, successful dependency.

Here are some key concepts that can help you improve the personal brand of your team:

- Make your brand's purpose clear, and something that employees will want to be a part of. The clearer the statement, the easier it is to participate.
- Help each employee discover what makes them a unique individual, and what they can offer their company.
- Give them a network for their voice. These people are your best brand advocates. Give them the tools to become that! Have an employee website, an employee-run blog, or social media pages where employees can share content among themselves, and with clients.
- Give them the spotlight. Make them involved in your business' events. Invite them to use social media, have them be speakers at keynote events, and to take over at conferences. Be proud of your team, and show them you have trust in them at the highest level.
- Make them want to improve their brand. Make them proud to be a part of your company, and want to share with the world just how great it is to be part of your business.

Don't forget about yourself. As an entrepreneur and marketer, you have to ensure your personal brand is being catered to, and improved. It will bring you success as well.

To summarize, improving your team's image is mutually beneficial. Employees feel better working in something they feel important in, and it will bring you greater business opportunities and success. Use the same techniques and mentality as with your brand, and apply it to its people.

Three essential questions to guide your team branding:

- How can my team enjoy more of the spotlight?
- How can we show off their unique skills and experiences, while simultaneously benefitting the company?
- How can we improve their personal brand, just as we'd improve ours?

Be proud of your team, they are your brand!

My first experience with leverage occurred when I was 15 years old. It began as I was marketing my own musical projects. One night, I discovered that I could monetize my YouTube music videos. So, my entrepreneurial instinct motivated me to try the service out.

The next morning, I noticed I had earned 0.50$ overnight. At the time, I felt like the world was my oyster. I had heard that great entrepreneurs make money in their sleep, but had never known what it felt like until that moment. Now, I felt it, and lived it; it didn't matter that the amount was so minimal.

I know, 0.50$ may not be much, but that morning was a learning experience for me: I knew what it meant to earn money doing what I enjoyed, and, from that point on, strived to achieve that same feeling of success.

Hard Work Does Not Necessarily Equal Results

The old adage is that, the harder you work, the better your results become. I find that incorrect; I believe that, the more leverage you have, the better the results. As marketers, we need to work smarter, instead of harder. We have this belief that the more hours we put in, the better the outcome will be. Unfortunately, the world won't give you 1 billion dollars because you worked hard, or "deserved it". The universe doesn't care. Only expect the big results when you're offering something of value.

Great marketers understand this.

Let me give you one simple example. You sell apple seeds. Lucky for you, you are the only one who sells apple seeds, so you get to sell them at your price. Do you believe you'd have to work hard for your business to succeed? Or, if you had the ability to make people rich by meeting with them for an hour; would you need to work for your money? No, because what you offer no one else can; its value is immeasurable.

Sadly, most entrepreneurs and marketers don't realize that results aren't proportional to the amount of work put in. Of course, working hard can help in many ways. But, it cannot be effective as long as it isn't combined with increasing value, and scalability.

Value

"If I had eight hours to chop down a tree, I'd spend six hours sharpening my ax."
— Abraham Lincoln

Value, by definition is the worth of something; how useful it is. The more you increase the value of something, the more it is worth. I'll write it again, because I want you to read it again. The more you increase the value of something, the more it is worth. Read it again and again; get it in your head.

When I started my consulting business, I was under the impression that the more hours I could work in a week, the richer I would be. So, I was working hard, finding new clients, consulting more, having Skype conferences, and having meetings. It felt good in the moment, but I was still working at the same rate week to week. I had effectively plateaued. I had no time to increase the value of my business. One day, I decided I'd break that plateau. I made a radical decision: I decided I'd be working 50% less. I used that 50% as time where I could invest in my brand's value. I spent more time reading books, going to seminars, meeting new people, growing my online audience, and getting my name on blogs. I did whatever I could to increase my brand's value, so that more people would want my services.

I believe that all marketers and entrepreneurs should master the skill of increasing value. If you own a clothing line, spend more time searching for quality fabric, and/or invest in building your brand and perceived value. If you are a personal trainer, spend more time making your personal brand and time valuable. Try to get media publications to talk about you, improve your skills as a trainer, grow an online audience, and participate in contests to win awards in your field. If you own a restaurant, work on your menu, and get more food reviewers through the door. Invite celebrities and local stars to eat for free, and make sure people know about it. Spend more time and money on training your chefs, work on their personal brands.

There are plenty of ways to improve the value (and perceived value) of what you market. Always ask yourself: how can I improve the value of my brand? When in doubt on certain business moves, think about how much value they could add to the brand. Base your decisions off of that.

Scalability

Our other best friend, scalability, is the ability to multiply revenue and sales, with a minimal increase in cost and resources. Selling the same product repeatedly, while being able to supply demand at the moment it is created, is the ultimate goal. A lot of business owners get stuck in situations where scalability is hard to accomplish. For example, personal services are less scalable, as we only have 24 hours in a day. Local businesses also suffer from less scalability. Their smaller range of business and their smaller inventory amounts make it harder to exploit scalability.

However, I believe that, regardless of the situation, that a brand can improve its scalability.

One method used to improve scalability is product building. Going back to our previous example with personal service providers, a wise move would be to spend less time providing services, and to start working on building information products. For example, a lawyer could package his most valuable documents and sell them as a product. Or, a make-up expert could sell video lessons on his/her website for a monthly fee.

Even restaurants, nightclubs, hotels, boutiques, and local businesses can improve their scalability by building products. For example, a restaurant could decide to market its menu as a cookbook, selling it on the Internet, or with a larger distribution. It could also decide to market one of its famous recipes in local or extended grocery chains.

Another way to improve scalability is the use of franchising and licensing. Businesses selling product use this strategy often, but it can also be used for services. One great example is Tony Robbins, with his life coaching services. In fact, he marketed the process he uses, and took the decision to franchise its coaching approach and brand. Since then, he's been able to charge more for his service, and earn passive income from franchisees.

There are multiple ways to improve scalability of your brand, and all they require is strategy and creativity. There is no predefined solution. A question I ask myself, or get my clients to ask themselves, when working on business scalability is: how could my brand help one billion people? Yes, scalability is seeing big, so don't be afraid to dream.

The goal is to help more people, with minimal increase in cost and time.

When increasing value and scalability work together, great brands are created.

Push-and-pull

Marketing is like flirting with someone: never come on too strong, but don't be afraid to present yourself. The concept I will be presenting this chapter is central on this idea; I call it the perfect "push and pull balance". When push strategies are perfectly balanced with pull strategies, expect new customers to come in like clockwork.

Marketing is about creating and keeping customers. To successfully create, then retain, customers, both push and pull strategies must be employed.

Push strategies are strategies that aim at taking the product straight to the customer. Some examples of push strategies are tradeshows, direct selling, prospecting, cold calls, and negotiating with retailers to distribute your product. I see it this way: push strategies are about finding the best way to get the product directly into the customers hands, without them seeking it out.

Pull strategies, as you might have deduced, is figuring out the best way to get the customer to seek out the product. In other words, creating demand. Some pull tactics include: advertising, public relations, endorsements and word-of-mouth.

When FUBU (A clothing brand founded by Shark investor Daymond John) started out, the brand decided to give clothes to famous rappers. They were given on the condition they were worn in video clips. This strategy was successful. It made customers want to buy the product, as their favourite celebrities were wearing it.

I give examples throughout this book of push and pull strategies. However, this chapter is to emphasize how important it is to utilize both strategies for optimal results. The reasoning is simple: push the product enough without enough demand, and negotiating prices and profit margins becomes difficult. Too much pull without push means less interested customers will receive your product.

For example, if you are a drink company, and set up a stand at an event, you will not sell much due to lack of demand. This lack of demand will lead you to discount your products. Say you are selling a B2B service. Most clients you contact will not be interested whatsoever if they have never heard of you.

On the other hand, creating too much demand without adequate means of buying makes customers go to competitors. It's like making someone hungry, then not providing them with food. I've seen so many brands and entrepreneurs create great interest in their brand, but never give the customer the opportunity to buy what they are selling.

It's all a case of supply and demand. As marketers, it's our job to ensure both are accounted for.

One perfect example of push and pull balance is with the pharmaceutical industry in 1997. The Food and Drug Administration decided to slack down the rules in drug advertising, thereby letting pharmaceutical brands advertise. Before that, they were only limited to "pushing" their products to doctors so they could prescribe it to patients. When they got the opportunity to create demand, with ads encouraging clients to talk to their doctor, overall prescription sales went up, from 700 million to more than 2.1 billion in four years. Pharmaceutical companies were now able to push their product to doctors through a complete distribution strategy, and able to "pull" customer by telling them to "ask for the product".

I already talk about how important it is to build awareness before product distribution. But, as the product is pushed to the customer, it is still important to constantly raise demand. Having a great pull strategy (creating interest) will help you in your selling efforts; having a great push strategy (getting your products in the hand of your customers) will ensure you consistently meet the demand you've created.

Make the customer hungry, and then sell him a plate of food.

Don't Discount Your Brand

I know, it's tempting. You have a product to sell. And, like always, you would like the sales numbers to be higher. So, to boost your numbers, you go down the route many marketers have gone before: "25% off all items for a limited time!"

Bad idea. It might pay off in the short-term, but you are withdrawing future, greater earnings for smaller, present ones.

Nancy Smith, founder and CEO of Analytics Partners, conducted a study. She analysed the impact of sales promotions over concerning different business on a global scale. The result? Sales promotion and discounts will train your customers to wait for promotions. It also reduces the perceived-value of your products. My point is, if the product is worth 100$, why would you be ready to sell it at 50$? In my opinion, it also makes the customer feel like the original 100$ price tag was a scam. If I bought something at 100$ and then see it for 50$ the next week, I'm definitely not buying from that vendor again for 100$.

You're probably wondering, "How do I give a push to my sales without sacrificing future earnings?" I'll get to that later.

What happened to JCPenney?

JCPenney, the giant American retailer, has fallen on hard times. They found themselves in a difficult position, thanks to a competitive industry and some bad strategic moves. So, what happened to put them in that situation? Many aspects lead to their struggles; however, I will be looking at a specific strategy.

JCPenney uses a strategy called High-low pricing. Basically, this strategy consists of initially selling a product at 100$, then dropping the price over time until, for example, 50$. As you can guess, most of the sales occur at 50$.

The problem with this strategy is that it made JCPenney lose its identity. There is a time that you entered the retailer and it was full of red tag. Should JCPenney want to sell a 400$ watch, all consumers were aware that if they waited, they could acquire the same watch for 150$. Also, the cheaper prices removed the prestige JCPenney held as an establishment. Any price-sensitive consumer will buy the watch for 150$, not 400$.

This lowers profits, and makes sales take much longer to take off.

So why not start selling it at 150$ right away? Of course, that would be a great idea. But, in a situation like JCPenney, the consumers would simply wait for the watch to drop MORE in price, to 75$. And we all understand that it's clearly not profitable to sell a 400$ watch at 75$.

Basic logic is: if you train your customers to wait for deals, they will always wait. You will slow down the sales process of price sensitive customers, and you will lower your prestige for wealthy consumers.

JCPenney got stuck in an infinite loop of deals.

In most cases, the best strategy is to find the perfect price for your own target market (not trying to please to everyone), and to stick with it. If your target can afford 1$, stick to 1$. If it can afford high end products like watches at 20 000$, stick with 20 000$.

So, let's get back to that quick "push" you want to give to your sales. The trick is to create promotions that don't involve price lowering. Keep in mind that promotions should be used scarcely. The most important thing about a promotion is the impact it creates.

A great example of a high-end brand making a great promotion is Bentley. Bentley, being a long-time partner with Breitling, decided to give exclusive Breitling watches to all buyers of the Continental ISR car in 2011. This marketing stunt was limited to 100 buyers only. They didn't slash the car's prices. Instead, they opted for a much more strategic move that not only boosted the brand's reputation as prestigious, but increased consumers' urgency to buy the car.

Footlocker has also made a smart move in the last few years. Instead of giving 50% on specific items, dragging down the perceived value of the product, they decided to give 50% off the second purchase for all in-store products. They called the campaign "Buy one, get one 50%". Though it is a promotion that plays on the price, it doesn't play on the value of single products. As a matter of fact, this promotion is constantly available, so customers won't think that buying later gives them an advantage. Plus, almost all products remain at full price, so the value is maintained across the store.

Hyundai is another good example. The automotive company used creative methods to make their promotions effective. They created a unique insurance plan: If someone bought a Hyundai, and lost their jobs, they would no longer need to pay off the car; they would own it. This dramatically boosted sales.

The fight for the lowest price is the fight for the biggest loser. So, don't bother trying to get in the ring. Instead, add value with your promotions. Make sure you don't get stuck in an infinite loop of deals all you gain are lost profits and less customers.

I will always remember when a good friend of mine told me: "Jules, it's normal to struggle. Life is just testing you to see if you deserve it."

Things can seem discouraging at times.

Life doesn't always go our way. We can't hope to climb Mount Everest without going through the process. You don't just reach the top after one jump. To succeed, we have to believe in ourselves; that we deserve the success, and that we deserve to reach the top.

Like the saying goes: "A smooth sea never made a skilled sailor."

Strive not for the smooth seas, but for the challenge that makes you a better person.

The Power of Storytelling

Ah, storytelling. A frequently discussed topic in the present world of marketing. What is storytelling? Simply put, storytelling (in the concept of marketing) is the art of joining powerful stories with your brand. The fun part of storytelling is its diversity; a story can be told from any part of your brand: its architecture, marketing campaigns, user experience, or in any touch points.

Storytelling is useful and effective. Studies have shown that the human brain retains information much more concretely if it has a strong emotion attached to it. If I asked you where you on September 11, 2001, I am sure that 95% of you will recall the memory vividly. I was 7 years old, and I remember it like it was yesterday. The reason for this was the emotional tug I felt on that day.

The thing about storytelling, and its power, is that it can be applied on a micro and macro level. It can be used as the marketer sees fit. Let me explain how it can be applied for each category:

Storytelling on a micro level is when it's used for specific strategies. For instance, it could be for a specific marketing campaign, for a website, for a specific product, or for any marketing material that your brand puts out there.

One great example of storytelling, on a micro level, is an advert Google produced for their search engine. Google produced a short, 3-minute movie about a man in India telling his granddaughter about his dear childhood friend. The woman then uses Google's search engine exclusively to find that friend, and arranges a meet up. By utilizing strong emotions, the purpose and power of the search engine is properly communicated. If you want to view this ad for yourself, search up "Google Search: Reunion".

Another powerful example of "micro" brand storytelling is The Lego Movie. This marketing move has been proclaimed as one of the most grandiose storytelling stunts ever orchestrated, in recent memory. Lego succeeded at promoting their products in what was, essentially, a glorified commercial. On top of that, clients paid to watch it! It definitely succeeded at not resembling an ad. The movie succeeded at not only reaching their target audience (families), but also created an emotional connection with them.

When looking to improve your brand's storytelling on a micro level, one method would be to polish up your brand's About Us page on its website (or any other area that houses an "About Us"). A short video describing the company, and its purpose, could also be made, then subsequently posted to social media and the brand's website. Storytelling can be implemented into any marketing strategy, so ask yourself: How can this medium bring about an interesting, emotional "tug" with my clients?

Storytelling on a macro level is, simply, to use the same storytelling across all aspects of your brand. Instead of using stories to promote your brand, the story is the core of your brand.

One strong example of macro brand storytelling is with Cadbury. They spread their story through every venue they can: TV ads, website, factory tours, and even theme parks. Instead of creating fictional storylines like many companies opt to do, they decided to use their own story; the founding of Cadbury. By doing this, Cadbury brought authenticity to the brand, and the feeling that people were actually buying from a significant company: a "real" piece of history.

The Walt Disney Company is another brand that uses storytelling across all channels to grow their brand. Customer Service workers will use the names of Disney characters when spelling something out ("M as in Mickey"), to make the client feel like they're still part of the "Disney Magic".

For truly astute storytelling, a mixture of both micro and macro practices should be adopted. Your story needs to be constant, and must be shared across ALL touch points. Ask yourself: is this strategy contributing to the storytelling of my brand? Is it helping my customer experience the story? Make sure reviews are done often, so updates or additions to various touch points can be completed. This way, all your customer interactions have the same underlying message.

If you want to improve emotional connection, loyalty and sales with current and prospective customers, storytelling is the way to go. Whether it is on a micro level, macro level, or both, it can only serve to be profitable.

The more you share your story with your clients, the more your brand will grow. Don't be afraid to be poignant!

Finding Your Perfect Price Point

Finding the perfect price for your product is never guaranteed. Let's be honest: the perfect price DOESN'T exist. There is no typo in the title. We won't be searching for the perfect price; we will be searching for YOUR perfect price. There are some important aspects you need to know to develop an effective pricing strategy. The topic of pricing point will be covered in two parts. The first section will show you the logical and technical aspects used to find your price; the next will cover some psychological aspects.

The Logical & Technical Price

Let's take, for example, that you are launching a new shoe brand which will be sold online. Naturally, you would want to find the perfect price. The equation for the perfect price, which is known as the traditional mark up formula, is as follows:

(Cost of production per unit + Cost of operations per unit) * Mark up % = Selling price

Let's say you plan on manufacturing a batch of 2500 shoes for your first year. It costs you 25 000$ of material and human resources (design, sewing, research). Your cost of production per unit is 10$. You plan on investing 10 000$ in marketing to sell them, and 10 000$ in exploitation costs and all other operating expenses (offices, accounting, employees). That comes out to 20 000$ in distribution costs (divided by 2 500 units) which gives a cost of 8 $ per unit. This brings you to a total of 18$ per shoes.

The standard in the shoe industry is a 100% mark up. Therefore, the selling price would be 36$, which would be technically perfect. Just don't start preparing price tags right away: the price isn't truly perfect yet.

The Marketing & Psychological Price

Now, 36$ is a good price on paper. It sets a base price for the product. But to improve the price, some factors need to be considered.

First, the competitors must be taken into consideration. In theory, you should have 3 immediate competitors that offer the same benefits and that are ranked at the same brand level (e.g. Nike and Adidas are on the same level. Lou Boutin and Louis Vuitton would be considered on the same level). Let's get back to the shoe brand. If you know your immediate competitors sell their shoes at 59$, then your benchmarking price is around 59$.

Now, reflect on the position you want in the marketplace. If you would want to be considered on a slightly higher brand level than your competitors (offering better quality and higher status than them), would you still sell your product at 36$ knowing your competitors sell their units at 59$? No, it would hurt your brand. This being said, a solution would be to double your selling price from 36$ to 79$. This would give your product a psychological advantage over your competitors'. You can then take the higher mark-up to invest more in marketing to sustain the brand perception you want, and invest more in quality products to offer concrete benefits.

Let's say, on the contrary, you would like to give the same value at a better price than your competitors. You recognize an area of the market that you can take advantage of with a lower price. Don't forget that you need to sell your shoes at MINIMUM 36$ to make a profit, and that your competitors sell them at 59$. This method requires that you remain at a lower price than your competitors, while keeping the same level of branding. A "winning" price would be selling your shoes at 39$ or 49$. Selling them at 39$ would be too close to your minimum price, which could make you fall to a lower brand/market level. This would give a "low quality-high price" stigma to your product (customers could perceive your product as competing with 24$ shoes instead of the targeted 59$). I would suggest that you instead sell them at 49$, which is still lower than your competitors, but doesn't bring your product to a lower brand level. This strategy would not necessarily make your brand perceived as better than your competitors. However, with good branding and marketing campaigns, gaining the perception of "same quality-better price" would win many customers over, due to their greater willingness to spend 49$ as opposed to 59$.

So, to sum up the steps of product pricing:

1. Determine the cost of producing your product and your operations, per unit.
2. Add an industry-standard mark-up. This will now be your minimum selling price.
3. Find the price point of at least 4 or 5 competitors that are on the same brand level to see the standard price range of your market. For example, avoid Rolex if you want to be a Timex competitor. Instead, benchmark your price with Timex, Adidas or Fossil.
4. Now, using the price point of your competitors, adjust your price slightly up or down depending on what perception you want over your competitors. Don't stray your price too far from the market standards, as you want to compete on the same brand level as your competitors.

I had been waiting for 38 minutes to get an answer. Finally, I heard a human voice, a customer service rep was talking to me. I was told I was on the U.S. line, and that I should be on the Canadian line. So, I asked to be transferred. The next person I spoke to was also from the U.S. line! So I, again, asked to be transferred.

When the third CS rep answered me, I politely asked if I was still on the U.S. line. All he answered was, "You still are."

He immediately hung up. To him, there was no risk; the company acts as separate entities per country.

So, to him, I wasn't worth his time.

I lost 45 minutes of my life. They lost a client.

Make Sure to Spend Time with Customers

An office is a dangerous place from where to see your brand. It's like scouting players for your team, but never actually going to see them play.

Not the most accurate metaphor, but the point is that it's ineffective. If you want to build a brand, you need to be in touch with the brand itself, while simultaneously managing it. That is why I recommend every marketer to spend at least one full day every month with customers. Whether it is as a salesman, sandwich artist, barista, waiter/waitress, or taking the place of any customer service employee. A lot of CEOs have started to do this, and it is a movement in the right direction. However, I do believe every Chief Marketing Officer, marketing director or anyone related to marketing in an organisation should do the same. The connection marketers establish with customers will motivate them to find brand new, innovative ideas.

Many companies use their growing size as an excuse to stop doing the little things that made them get there initially; this is wrong. How do you want to market a brand to customers you don't even know? Of course, you have a customer support team in charge of complaints. They also handle customer recommendations, which the marketing team utilizes. In order to take the next step, however, one must not know what customers want (which is the use of complaints and recommendations), but who the customers ARE.

This is basic logic: the more you know your customers, and interact personally with them, the better the marketer you become for your brand. It will help you excel in decision-making. As a matter of fact, getting involved in the field with actual customers will help you not only to understand your customers better, but will also give you plenty of new product ideas and features for existing products. It's also very refreshing to take a break from the office. It will help you change your mindset, and could lead to ground-breaking innovations in the long term. From a HR perspective, it will also be motivating for the employees to see the "corporate guy" working with them!

Alex Turnbull, CEO of Groove, decided to make the move. Even with a busy schedule as CEO of a highly growing start-up, he decided to spend at least 20 hours every week doing customer service. Sharing his experience on his personal blog, Alex Turnbull realized that by doing so, he would actually feel the needs of his customers.

"But when I was forced not only to own customer complaints, but to look into them and respond to an upset customer, I'd feel their pain on a much deeper level. An issue that might have otherwise been another task on the stack became a burning pain that was hurting a customer I was interacting with directly."

- Alex Turnbull, CEO at Groove

Up to now, his company Groove is earning more than 140 000$ in revenue every month.

Sujan Patel, VP of marketing at "When I Work" also decided to make the move into spending more time with customers when he was working at Bridge.us. By deciding to join the customer support team at his company, Sujan Patel was able to improve sales conversions by more than 250%. As a matter of fact, getting his feet wet with the customer support team gave him an insider look at how he could improve user experience and even write better ads. He did this by finding the perfect tone of voice for the brand and what customers wanted to hear to be in love with the product.

Put yourself in the shoes of a restaurant chain's marketing director. You decide to make the jump, and become a waiter in one of your locations one day, every week. For example, while serving customers, you could hear a joke that some customers repeat often when ordering food. This joke could actually become part of your next advertising campaign! Also, when customers think about what they want to eat, they might say that they did not really know what to order. This could lead to the idea of implementing sampling options to the menu. This idea could generate a lot of word of mouth, and improve the brand experience your brand offers. Trust me on this: you will get many ideas.

I am a firm believer that marketing is more about instinct and decision making than planning; getting an emotional and direct connection with your customers will help you become the best marketer you can be.

We all know that you start thinking and acting like the people you spend the most time with; you grow with them. So passing more time with your customers will help you a lot as a marketer, since you, and your brand, will grow with them. That can make the difference between being a good marketer, and a great one. There's no pride in managing your brand from an impenetrable corporate fortress.

So, go get your feet wet!

It Pays to Say Thank You

Did you know that it cost 5 times more to find new clients than to keep the ones you have right now? And that it also costs 5 times less to get new clients from referrals than from advertising? I'm not saying that advertising should not be a part of your marketing strategy; I'm saying that you should invest in customer loyalty and referrals. Here are two tricks that can improve customer retention, loyalty and referrals.

Ask for a referral and say THANK YOU

Happy customers are willing to refer you to their friends. But sometimes they are busy, and they forget about it. Here's the simplest trick to ensure they refer: Just ask for one.

There is nothing wrong with saying (For the sake of the example, the fictional client will be called John) "thanks a ton for your business

John, would you mind referring us, and talking about our business to your friends? We work very hard to satisfy customers like you, and every referral is sincerely appreciated."

In other words, train your employees to show appreciation for the customer's service whenever they're able to. The customer will feel close to you, and everyone loves to talk about businesses that they feel they have a special relationship with. The effect will be remarkable.

Businesses are so busy figuring out marketing ideas to increase brand loyalty and referral amounts that they forget about simply asking.

Give them THANK YOU gifts (or why loyalty programs are not good)

Forget loyalty programs. Would you tell a friend, "every time you call me you get a point, and after 20 points I will buy you a restaurant meal!" No, you wouldn't. So why would you do it for your customers? In some cases it can be interesting, but don't forget that people want to do business with people they feel they can be friends with.

I'll tell you an anecdote. There is a small sushi place around where I live. I was going there maybe 2-3 times per month. I didn't have a preference for the place, its location just was beneficial. Yes, the sushi was great, but there are other places you can find great sushi.

Then, one day, the owner came to see me while I was eating, and said "THANK YOU Jules, I know you come here a lot and I wanted to thank you for your business. Here are 3 free sushi rolls for you, enjoy them."

That's it, that's all he needed to say. It cost him nothing to say it, and maybe 3 dollars to give me the sushi. But, he had my loyalty now. He didn't ask for nothing in return, he didn't ask me to come 12 more times so I can get the same offer. He just gave it to me, like it was a gift, from one friend to another. No strings attached. After that, he EARNED my loyalty.

Ever since then, I go there twice a week and I talk about this place to my friends.

Lesson: Say thank you, and give without asking back. Your customers will give you their loyalty in return.

Follow up two weeks later

Businesses, marketing managers and sales directors are still thinking with an old, "funnel" mentality. The best way to see it now is as a marketing "cloud". Once they buy from you, they go back into the cloud. It's a circular idea. Your goal is to have them come back.

To sum it all up: Marketers are so busy looking for new customers that they tend to forget the best ones: the customers they already have.

Here's a simple question: Are you following up on your customers 2 weeks after a sale?

If you are doing it, keep on doing it!

If you are not doing it, start doing it right now. Consider it urgent.

Let's say you sell shoes for a shoe brand. You sold a pair to a customer called John. So here is something you can say once it'll have been 2 weeks since the initial sale:

Hi John, how are you?

Thank you very much for your last sale. We wanted to follow up with you to ask how you are enjoying your new pair of shoes. Is it everything you wanted for your shoe needs?

We also wanted to call to say thank you. If there is anything we can do to help you, just let us know.

Thanks again.

Customers will love it, especially if you are selling a high-end brand or service. You will be remembered by them.

Therefore, say thank you. Embrace the feeling of being grateful to your customers. Integrate the idea of going out of your way to say "thank you" to your marketing strategy. Train your employees for it. Train yourself for it.

Customers will love it and it will pay off.

Thank you!

The Drug Dealer Strategy

Let me preface this by specifying that I'm not encouraging you to become a drug dealer. My point is that, both in real life and in popular culture/media, drug dealers have been known to give out free samplings of their product. Essentially, drug dealers believe in their product enough to give it away for free.

The rule is simple: Never charge first time customers. It not only increases brand loyalty, but also improves trust, brand awareness and word of mouth.

It's logical: if you see the "new-era" sales ideology as a cloud more than as a funnel, you have a solid repeat business strategy, a top-quality product, and that you targeted the proper target market, why would you be afraid to give away your product for free initially?

You're already confident in everything surrounding it.

Redbull follows this strategy with their Red Bull Girls/Wings scheme. They travel around the most populated cities, giving away free redbulls. They attend the biggest events in those cities, and give away their product for free. Over the last years, it has grown their brand and helped them conquer new markets, hereby increasing loyalty in their customer base. By giving away free products (even to frequent customers), it builds a sort of "momentum" for the customer, something I call the "Redbull-Habit".

Freshbooks, the accounting/book keeping software for small businesses, follows this strategy by offering a free 30 day trial period. Neil Patel, an Internet marketing leader, performed a test: offering a free trial resulted in improving the revenue of one of his membership programs by 27%. There are many software products doing this, and there is a reason behind that: it pays and converts. Offering a free 30 day trial increases trust, and influences the buyer; it's a no-brainer to try something for free. Also, when you have a customer going through the trial, they tend to grow accustomed to the product's presence. When the trial ends, the customer will feel obliged to purchase, due to how frequently it was used towards the end of the 30 days.

Another story of someone using the Drug dealer strategy is Seth Godin with his book, called

Unleashing the Ideavirus. He wrote it in 12 days, then went to see his publisher and said: "I want this book to come out right away, but I want to also give it away for free on my blog". The publisher said no. So, Seth decided to put it up for free on his website as an eBook, and to self-publish it on Amazon for $40.

I don't mean you are obligated to give away your TOTAL product for FREE. What about a sample? For example, if you are selling a book, giving the first 25 pages away might hook customers into buying the full product. If you are marketing a clothing brand, why not give out free accessories, like wristbands and sunglasses, marketing your brand? If you market a new pasta sauce, can you partner with local food stores to make a weeklong promotion, where free sauce samples are given to every customer?

Go ahead; have fun brainstorming and improving your drug dealer skills. Keep in mind: The more you give, the more you earn. Let them taste your magical concoction of marketing and product excellence.

What will come will come, and we'll meet it
when it does.
— Hagrid

Do not judge this quote based on its provenance;
it still has its significance. Reading that quote
helps me realize how much I would tend to
overthink in the past, trying to control the future
when I cannot even control the weather for
tomorrow.

I kept wasting my time trying to connect dots
that hadn't even come to exist yet. Because I
couldn't map my future, I would never take any
steps forward; I thought I would eventually
have a "Eureka!" moment, which would make
everything clear. All this did was bring me fear,
and resistance to embrace change. It stopped me
from acting, it stopped me from loving, and it
stopped me from, most important of all, living. I
am not saying the future should never be
addressed. I am able to think about the future
peacefully, because I focus on the present. I
realize the future is a beautiful mystery, and that
it will always remain unknown. I'll figure it out
once the future becomes my present. I am not
afraid of repercussions; after all, progress can
only be experienced now, not later.

I thought I could see tomorrow. In reality, I look
at today, and ensure my better tomorrow.

Releasing the shackles of fear is something
everyone, marketer or otherwise, needs to
accomplish, in order to truly succeed.

Long-Term Plans Are Useless

Go ahead; throw them away! The only use for such plans is when you need to present one to someone, such as a bank, investors, or strategic partners. Other than that, you can throw them away.

For the purpose of this section, I'm defining "long-term plans" as plans that are for a significant chunk of the future; 12 months, or more.

Marakon Associates, in collaboration with the Economist Intelligence Unit, surveyed 156 top executives at companies that record over one billion in sales annually. Out of those 156 executives, only 11% believed that long term strategic planning was worth the effort. The rest believed that it was an obstacle to great decision-making and execution. Yet, long-term plans are a staple for many businesses. This survey led the

Harvard Business Review to determine that decision-making is something far more important than long-term planning. The same applies to marketing.

Can you tell me the weather 12 months from now? If, 12 months ago, you tried to predict your company's success, would any plan be able to accurately foresee it? Or, if you tried to determine today's marketing trends 12 months ago, would you have been accurate? Probably not.

But, that doesn't mean strategy is useless. Instead, we should see strategy as a tool for strong decision-making, instead of a tool for long-term planning. When you are planning for the long-term, you are effectively giving yourself tunnel vision. You create a hypothetical goal, and focus purely on that. Strategy, market research and competitor analysis are crucial to grow your brand. In fact, in order to make great decisions and execute with awesome results, we need to give ourselves tools to do so. It will not only sharpen your vision, but it will help your day-to-day decisions.

Recently, more start-ups and top brand executives have been leaning towards a much more proactive method of management. The formula is simple: create that "big picture" view, then plan in the short term, then execute right away. In today's business world, things change at a nearly instant rate. This factor effectively nullifies long-term planning.

Donald trump, the real estate mogul, wrote this passage in one of his books: "Keep the big picture in mind while attending to the daily details". This has helped me for the last few years. Once the vision is crystal clear for you and the management team, it is time to act and execute to get there. Simple as that.

Of course, planning can help you solve steps that must be taken to reach your goal.

I've come to believe that the perfect timeline for planning lasts 90 days. It becomes much easier to sprint, when the finish line is in view. Planning becomes much easier once the goal is clearly visible. 90 day planning is clearer, less time consuming, while still allowing time to make adjustments. Don't trap yourself in a long-term plan that doesn't reflect your current situation adequately. As Mark Zuckerberg loves to say, "Move fast and break things"!

I tend to prefer to keep a big-picture goal in my mind, without sticking to a complex plan to get there. I try to keep my life, and my business, as simple as possible; I have prepared my environment with this in mind. I focus on execution, which gives my day-to-day a motivating momentum.

Here are some key points to help you become a short-term planning and execution Jedi:

- Do tons of research – Become obsessed with market trends, new marketing strategies, new social platforms, analysing your competitors, and any other informative tool. Replace time spent on planning, with research and analysis. It will open your eyes, help you become the best marketer for your brand, and give you the tools for great decision-making and strategy.
- Have a clear vision for your brand – Holding your vision close to all operations will allow you to execute and have better results. Great visions are timeless. You might want to become the leading company in a particular domain, or to solve a problem plaguing billions of people. Visions are akin to dreams, and marketers are dreamers. Strategic dreamers.
- Develop a simple 90 day plan – don't pay attention to details, it's meant to resemble a guideline. Figure out where you want your brand to be in 90 days, and note it down. Keep it simple, with key goals, strategies, steps, and metrics. You need to be able to analyse results, so make sure the plan, and its goals, can be easily quantified. See this plan as one step in the staircase that is the path to your vision.
- Execute – 80% of your time should be given to executing. This is where results happen. Once your 90 day plan is done, put it aside and focus on making things happen; your plan is what allows this to

pay off. Also, keeping yourself proactive and always in an execution mode is more motivating. It keeps a solid tempo to your life. Make sure you keep an open mind, and change your plan if needed.

I've met many entrepreneurs that have built successful businesses without business plans. I've met plenty of marketers that grew successful brands without marketing plans. In fact, Anthony K. Tjan, a business author and expert, conducted a survey regarding businesses that had a successful exit, such as an IPO, or a sale to another company. The results were astonishing: 70% of those businesses did not start with a business plan. Instead, they focused on strong decision-making, and on executing in the short-term. They reached milestones that were never expected in the long-term. Therefore, dump your long-term plan. Focus on execution, and enjoy the ride to growing and marketing your brand.

Make things happen! Become the marketer that will make or break your brand.

The World is Not a Market

I often hear entrepreneurs and clients say that everybody is in their target market, and that every industry is their playground. Hearing this never ceases to amaze me. It has been consistently proven: the smaller the niche, the better the results. So, when it comes to developing a product or a marketing strategy, make sure you are narrowing your niche as much as you can. Many entrepreneurs think that by doing so they will lose customers. It's actually the opposite; you will gain new ones. You can't be everything to everyone.

Here are two concepts that will help you better understand how you can narrow your niche when launching a new product, or focusing the niche of your current product. It's never too late. Ideally, for the most effective niche strategy, using these two concepts simultaneously is recommended.

The offer focus

The offer focus is all about making the focus of your offer and product more accurate. The concept is simple: become the best at one thing. For example, if you own a shampoo brand, could you become the leader in men's shampoo? Pushing that even further, could you become the leader in men's sport/athletic shampoo? The target market would be big enough to make solid revenue, it would be a lot easier to market, and word-of-mouth would be triggered easily. The product would also not be seen as a "jack-of-all-trades" product; instead, it would be seen as a quality product of high value.

If you are marketing a coffee brand, could this brand focus only on dark and strong coffee? Pushing it further again, could this coffee focus on dark and strong coffee made with biological beans? Or could you focus only on high priced coffee? Too many companies try the "jack-of-all-trades" route. Successful entrepreneurs realize that for their company to be great, it must attain a specific audience.

The horizontal & vertical market in B2B

This concept is normally used in technology, or B2B marketing, but it is very important to know for every kind of marketer. Of course, B2B needs strong branding too. But this concept is also very helpful in B2C.

Vertical market is when you cater to multiple needs of a specific industry, regardless of the size of the business. Marketing an all-in-one client management software that is specialized for the medical industry is an example of a vertical strategy. Another example would be offering various marketing consulting services specialized purely for the banking industry.

A horizontal market, on the other hand, is when you offer a specific product or technology, but to a very large audience/industry. A good example would be offering web design services that are only for large corporations, regardless of their industry. Another example would be marketing a book-keeping software to small businesses and entrepreneurs exclusively, as Freshbooks does perfectly.

So now, whether you are marketing a new startup or product, ask yourself: Can I narrow the niche of my product and what it offers? Or can I narrow my focus exclusively towards a vertical market?

If you are currently marketing an already launched product, gather data and analyse it. For example, if you see that the highest paying clients, and the ones you enjoy the most working with, are in a specific industry, maybe it's time to focus on serving this industry and becoming a leader with your specified product! Or, if you own a product and see that 85% of men are using your product, maybe it's time to focus on men's only marketing and product strategies.

Sometimes, the product niche will be found on its own. But to be certain you are maximizing results, always strive to narrow your niche.

Play with those concepts to narrow your product's focus. Remember, marketing is fun!

What's your position?

How are you different from your competition? When asking yourself this, only one or two words should be said. If, for the rest of your brand's days, your brand name would change for the word best representing it, what would it be? Or, when asked about your brand or company, you would only be able to say ONE or TWO words. What would they be? This is the simplest way to explain positioning.

Of course, positioning a brand and a business can be much more complicated; and can involve more analysis and development. But, in a nutshell, positioning is how you are different from the competition.

As mentioned before, brand positioning can involve a large amount of evaluation. However, these extra complications are unnecessary, especially when the key words you are looking for are unknown to you.

I've tried brand positioning myself. I've given 20 of the world's top brands some words that I believe describe them best.

- Apple: Different & Innovative;
- Walt Disney: Magic;
- Samsung: Innovation;
- Volvo: Safety;
- BMW: Driving Experience;
- Mercedes: High-end;
- Drake: Emotions;
- Malboro: Manly;
- Porsche: Performance;
- Rolex: Luxurious;
- Timex: Affordable Quality
- H&M: Low priced & fashion;
- Redbull: Energy & Pushing the limits;
- Facebook: Friendship;
- American Express: Exclusive-only;
- Virgin Group: Challenging the conventional;
- FedEx: Express & Overnight;
- Blackberry: Business (But they lost it, sadly);

One case study that I like is FedEx. Early in their brand's existence, their positioning was: "We have trains, trucks and planes". The positioning was vague, and lacked the poignancy that one or two words hold. The company was struggling to become an industry leader. Later on, they changed their positioning, giving their brand the reputation of excelling at "overnight" delivery.

Multiple marketing efforts and campaigns like their slogan "When it absolutely, positively has to be there overnight." helped them sharpen their positioning. Over time, people started to say "I'll FedEx that to you," when they wanted to say that they would ship it in express to get it to their recipient the next day. Their positioning started to shift from something not really clear, to the word "overnight, or express". Until now, they've kept this strategy and it has guided them, ensuring they stay an industry leader.

With the competition getting increasingly intense in this business world, make sure your brand is different from the competition. If you can't accurately find what distinguishes your brand from others, you will struggle now, and in the future.

If you wanted your brand to be SYNONYMOUS with one word, what would that word be?

Find that word.

Price Anchoring Strategy

In this chapter, I will now introduce a strategy that adds VALUE and IMPACT to your perfect price. This strategy is known as Price Anchoring. I've come up with a simple sentence to sum up the anchoring strategy:

The best way to sell something at 50$ is to sell something at 80$.

Here are some examples of price anchoring. Look over and analyze each; try to notice a pattern. Then, I'll explain the significance of each example.

1.

Gold plan: 990$ / month
Silver plan: 290$ / month
Bronze plan: 99$ / month

This first example is simple. Let's say your goal is to sell 290$ / month memberships. If you add variety to the product and include a 99$/ month membership on top of the 290$/month membership, you can be sure that people would choose the 99$/ month membership. People avoid extremes. Now, let's say you want to boost the sales of your 290$ / month membership. The solution? Add a 990$ / month membership, even if you know you'll barely sell any copies of it. This will simply make the 290$ / month membership seem cheaper, and more valuable simultaneously. Again, people tend to avoid extremes. They will not lean towards the cheapest or most expensive membership; instead gravitating towards the middle, 290$ / month membership. This example is ideally made for online membership programs.

2.

Small beer: 1,60$
Medium beer: 1,80$
Large beer: 2,50$

This example is best applied in restaurant or bar pricing. Let's say you want to sell a beer or an entrée at 1.80$. The best way to maximize your sales numbers with that specific item would be to offer it in 3 different sizes. The smallest at 1.60$, the target sale price at 1.80$, and a larger one at 2.50$.

By doing that, emphasis is placed on the medium (your targeted price) size.

Psychologically, people would tend to think: The smaller size isn't large enough to satisfy a craving, and it's almost the same price as the medium item. Plus, the large item is too expensive to warrant a purchase. This would give the medium sized item the appearance that it is a "smart purchase", boosting its sales. Mentally, the customers would feel like it's a no-brainer to go with the medium size. As a bonus, having multiple sizes would pander to a wider audience. As with drinks, someone who is really thirsty would be inclined to buy the large, and vice versa for the small.

3.

Basic plan: 25$ / month
Premium plan: 37,50$ / month
Premium annual plan: 375$ / year

This is an example I prefer to utilize when developing a new price with my clients. One method of adding impact and value to a price is changing its presentation. For example: you sell a monthly package at 37.50$ (which comes out to 450$ / year). You could offer to sell it for a annual fee of 375$ along with the aforementioned monthly price. Despite it being technically a smarter purchase, customers will assume the monthly price is cheaper, due to the low, per-month fee. Now, presentation isn't only different prices. Pricing metrics can also affect the perception of price. For example: choosing price annually instead of monthly, price per unit instead of price per year, etc. Take my product, for instance. My product has annual prices, along with a lifetime price, that's three times the annual fee. There have been clients who have purchased the product; however, they only represent 3% of my online sales. My goal is to use this package to make my annual fee seem more attractive.

Here are the key steps for a simple Price Anchoring strategy:

1. Choose the item you want to sell the most, that you consider has the best value;
2. Sell something a little bit cheaper, but with much less benefits;
3. Make sure that it is presented in comparison to the item you want to sell the most;
4. Now, inversely to step 2, sell something at a much higher price, with very good benefits.
5. Make sure that you also present this item and price in comparison to the one you want to sell the most.
6. Poof! Suddenly, your target product will seem much more valuable to consumers, and the product wasn't modified in the slightest!;
7. Watch the target product's sales grow.

I hope this strategy will allow you to bring your product's impact and value to the next level.

My friend from New York gave me this snippet of advice: "If you want a piece of the pie, buy property in NYC. Then, watch what the rich are doing; copy them."

What he told me may apply perfectly to real estate. However, I believe it also applies to life. If you want to succeed like the successful, study them. Emulate them, and obsess after their success. You want the same thing they have, and they are showing you how to get it. Lackadaisical work will bring you nowhere.

You have to become the successful, in every sense of the word. Your attitude will translate into results.

Location, Location, Location

They say location is everything. They're not wrong: it is everything... and great marketers know that. Before all this newfangled "marketing", there was one key point in business success: location. In fact, your location was the only way for you to succeed in the marketplace. Back when the marketplace was, quite literally, a place.

Still, marketers and entrepreneurs tend to forget that nowadays. They think that a bigger advertising budget and a great product will compensate for a subpar location, which is false. Of course, you can have success even if location is a handicap. But, as your business grows, a great location won't be an option if you desire greater success.

What is location?

Location is not just for retail or physical shops. Location is the "Place" in the 4P marketing mix (Place, price, product, promotion). It includes all distribution channels, delivery services, physical boutiques, Google search result priority, online stores, and even domain names for online businesses. It is, basically, where your product first meets its customers.

I heard a story, some months ago, that reminded me of the importance of location in marketing. A good friend of mine told me that, several years ago, an important pharmacy chain in New York decided to sell all the locations they had that were not on a corner, then bought more locations that were on corners. This move cost them a fortune, the amount of which was insignificant to them; they were thinking long term. The strategy behind this move was simple: by being on street corners, they were being seen by double the people. It was fitting for their environment: in a high traffic place like New York City, where you don't necessarily have the time to get your iPhone to look up the nearest pharmacy, being on a street corner is the best way to ensure people will take notice of the pharmacy. Either by walking past it, or noticing it from afar. To the pharmacy chain, it was akin to owning two separate stores.

That anecdote made me realize that location is everything, and that optimizing it can be crucial for your brand. For example, what is the point of building word of mouth, or advertising campaigns, if your target market never gets a chance to be in the right proximity to buy your product? What's the point of telling a hungry man that you have a burger if you are two states away from him?

Another story strengthened my understanding of the importance of location. I am a sushi lover, and this sushi restaurant was running a local advertising campaign in my town. They probably invested a lot of money to have sushi aficionados, like me, gain interest in their product. For a couple of weeks, they nurtured my hunger for sushi; every time I heard their ads, I went to eat sushi. Only thing: I went to eat sushi someplace else. Unfortunately, I realized that this particular sushi place was 30 miles away from where I do the majority of my work, and they didn't offer delivery. So every time I heard the ad, I gave my sushi dollars to someone else. If I was a consultant for them, I would tell them right away to offer delivery services or to stop running ads around all the region. The first option would cost them more, but they would get three times more business; the second option would reduce their ad expenses and improve campaign results.

This being said, every brand can optimize its location strategy. I have developed a series of question that you can ask yourself, as a brand owner, so you can improve your strategy. These questions will also give you some examples of what you could do as "templates" for optimizing your location.

- If you own an online clothing brand, could you buy more domain names redirecting to your original domain? That way, more people can "end up" on your website. Or, could you offer free shipping, so people will choose to buy online instead of somewhere else? Another idea would be selling on other websites.
- If you're trying to sell your first book, could you make it be a product in five different online retailers? Local bookstores are a good idea as well. Maybe even both?
- If you own a restaurant, can you offer delivery? Or can you follow the "pop-up" model and arrange a pop-up restaurant or a food truck at high-traffic events? Pop-up shops are an effective medium in many other industries.
- If you are a consultant, could you build a package to deliver consultation services over the phone (or other long-distance services, such as Skype) nationwide, instead of sticking with local visits?
- If you own a sporting goods boutique, could you start selling online? Or can you launch a new shop in a town close to your current location?
- If you own an established construction company, would you franchise the brand? Establishing partnerships with other

companies in other areas could also reach a larger clientele, faster.

- If you own a local garage, could you move your current location to a much more high-traffic area, where people will drive by you more often?
- If you own a mobile iOS app, could you port it to other operating systems? Computer ports are also a method to reach new clients. Also, trying to boost the apps rating will make it easier for shoppers to stumble across it while shopping for applications.
- If you are renowned for a particular ability, partnering with a company to exploit that talent could reach more people (Gordon Ramsay endorsed steaks, for example).

Of course, these were just fictional businesses. These ideas can be made to your image, as you see fit. As you can see, every business and brand can improve its location strategy. You just need to be creative and strategic about it. Think long-term revenue rather than short-term revenue.

Let's get this straight: chances are that people won't travel cross-country, or even across town, to buy your product; make it as accessible as possible. Locate what you are selling in the vicinity of your target market's daily life: be it their commute to work, or even their website browsing habits.

Think Inside the Box

Yes, you read that right. You should never try to think outside the box. In fact, great "outside the box" ideas come from thinking inside of it. As much as great product innovations come from products that already exist in the market place, great ideas come from applying a tried-and-true method to something no one would have thought of applying it to.

There is a great quote that I like to cite when I am trying to explain this concept to my clients, or people I'm discussing with.

"Don't reinvent the wheel, just realign it."
— Anthony J. D'Angelo

This is so powerful. We tend to think that innovations are something of a myth, and that only savants such as Jobs or Zuckerberg can make them a reality. On the contrary: innovation can be made reality by anyone.

Let's reflect for a moment. Is the iPod that different from the Walkman? Is the iPhone any different than the iPod? Is the Computer so different from the Commodore, and the MacBook Pro from the computer? Is Facebook really different than Myspace? Or is the single-serve coffee machine really different from a regular coffee machine? You get the point. Those innovations all started from existing ideas.

It is against human nature to think outside the box. It is often considered foreign, and scary. However, that does not mean an inside the box idea cannot be seen as an outside the box one. That's how you will trick your mind to finding those elusive innovations; by letting your mind think that those ideas come from within that box. That's how you will be able to get the best innovative marketing ideas. I am pretty sure that some people will disagree with me, but I am not here to appeal to popular opinion: Inside the box is where you will be creative. The great thing about this is that everyone can think inside the box. Therefore, you have no reason to say you "can't get any ideas".

Let me "freestyle" an example here for you.

Let's say, you want to get new ideas for a marketing campaign for your energy drink brand. Instead of starting from scratch, why not start from your last successful campaign?

Another idea would be to start with a campaign that you loved from a world-leading brand. This might be the case if you've never really made a real marketing campaign, so you decide to start with an existing top-brand campaign. For the sake of the example, you choose the Doritos Advertising Contest from Doritos (For good examples of advertising, checking these out on YouTube is recommended).

Now, the Doritos campaign idea is inside your box. And you can play inside this box.

There's a good chance that you don't have the same budget and audience as Doritos, so you probably need to do it on a "smaller scale". For example, instead of doing the contest with video ads, you now decide to do it on Instagram with a photo campaign under a specific hashtag.

Now you realize that this type of campaign is "Déjà Vu". You want to do it a little bigger; you want to add a little "wow" factor to it. So, you now decide that the winning picture will be the packaging for the next 10 000 bottles distributed. That idea now twists the whole campaign; instead of doing photo ads, your audience needs to take a photo that would make a great creative packaging label and they need to post it under their own Instagram account, again with a specific hashtag.

You now have a pretty cool campaign! Imagine if you had started by trying to look outside of the box; you would probably still be wondering how to get out of it.

But, don't stop there. Start again, do the same process, but with other ideas in your box. Generate other ideas for that campaign. Try to generate at least 10 great ideas. After that, mix those ideas. Put those ideas in a new "box". After a bit of mixing, you'll get that "Outside of the box" idea you were looking for, and every ingredient of that idea will have come from inside the box!

Let's say, you are creating a new product line. You need a new name for it. Following the same process, instead of trying to find outside of the box names, you would start with the existing names of products lines you have. Those names would be in your box. You could also add product names in this box from other brands that you love. Starting with your own names would not only help you generate new ideas, but that would also give your product continuity compared to your other products; thus helping your whole brand succeed.

The same process applies for generating new products, features, and ideas. In your box, you could put your current product features, competitors' product features, features you love from another different industry, and ideas from new market trends. Now, mixing this "salad bowl" of ideas will allow you to come up with an entirely new one.

You can use the same process when generating new ideas for product innovation, brand names, and packaging designs. In other words, you can use this process every time you need new ideas.

Have fun using boxes!

Put Your Boxing Gloves On

The majority, if not all of you, have probably seen the "I'm a Mac/PC" advertisements. Most of you know about Coke and Pepsi's continuous ad war, or the constant clashing of FedEx and UPS.

If any of these do not ring a bell, I highly suggest researching on the following topics:

- Mac vs Pc ads
- Coca-Cola vs Pepsi Ads
- FedEx vs UPS ads
- McDonald vs Burger King ads

Researching these yields interesting results.

These "attack" ads are not meant to be purely egotistical power trips for Fortune 500 companies. Much thought goes into these campaigns, it is a calculated move. These marketing fights have two major benefits: improving your brand positioning in relation to your competitors, and increasing word-of-mouth. Consumers enjoy seeing companies duke it out through advertisements, as it breathes life into the brands. There is a reason reality shows are so popular; consumers find drama addicting. Friendly conflict between brands is a good way to nab consumers' attention.

The fight will create a divide among consumers, making your clients even more loyal to your brand. Since the Apple vs PC ads, consumers have been arguing on both sides, with people vehemently avoiding anything originating from the other brand. These campaigns create brand advocates, that work for you for free. People love taking sides, and being part of a collective. Use your brand to answer that need.

This practice is something often seen in the music and professional sports industries, particularly boxing.

Don't focus on one type of opponent. You could pick a fight with an entire industry. Your campaign doesn't need to seldom use advertising. In fact, there are plenty of ways you could put your boxing gloves on as a brand. Here are some examples:

- Making a reference to something your brand does better, or differently, than your competitors, in an interview setting.

The media would be happy to talk about it, and give you word-of-mouth.

- Your brand's website could detail in what ways it separates itself from its competitors. Making humoristic jabs at other brands can be effective.

- Making the clash between brands the heart of your brand's positioning is another viable option. For example, Avis decided to pick on Hertz, as they were number one in the nation. It completely changed their positioning, focusing on communicating to customers why people should choose Avis instead of Hertz. It has been a huge success.

- Starting any sort of clash on social media, such as Twitter, is simple, free, and quick. It would get people talking right away.

As you can see, there is no definite way on how you should conduct this marketing fight. Just be creative, mature, and intelligent. The goal is to become "fight-ready", and to always have your boxing gloves on as marketers. This way, you will be alert for clashing opportunities, and be completely knowledgeable on what to do in those upcoming situations.

So whom are you going to fight? Put your boxing gloves on, and improve your positioning, brand loyalty, and word-of-mouth.

Just like every fight, however, make sure not to hurt yourself. Also, it is imperative to stay respectful. Marketing fights are akin to boxing matches, not street fights.

Write it in one Sentence

My goal, when starting this book, was to have entrepreneurs and businesspeople become better marketers, by seeing marketing from a non-traditional perspective. Notice I wrote this in one sentence, and how effective it was at delivering its intended message.

Last night, I was at a formal cocktail evening, and I asked someone: "so, what do you do?" I've already explained how people love to talk about themselves, so you can see where this is going. He started talking. And then, he kept going. And going. As expected, he lost me.

I am not saying that what he's doing is bad; not in the slightest! In fact, it looked like something very interesting and that was solving a need. But, his explanation of it was too long. Don't you realize? I could have been the next Mark Cuban (a Shark Tank investor) searching for the next

Apple, and his product could actually have been what I was looking for. Due to the length of his speech, there's no chance of that happening.

Based on my experience, decision makers have a short attention span. Customers are decision makers. They decide if they will spend one single penny on you or not. So, whether you are trying to make a business deal with a strategic partner, or you are trying to make a sale, you are talking to a decision maker.

Breaking news: Decisions are triggered by emotions more than rationality. In fact, several years ago, Antonio Damasio, a Portuguese-American neuroscientist and neurobiologist, demonstrated that most of our decisions as humans are based on emotions, rather than logic. This being said, it's no secret nowadays that it's more effective to talk about missions and purposes, as opposed to benefits and features. We always have time to look at the features and product benefits once the magic hooks us.

Don't forget that, over time, features can change. However, the mission stays forever. Your mission can evolve, but it must remain timeless. Technologies, trends, and customer needs keep changing everyday; don't hurt yourself by being known exclusively for a "feature". Instead, try to make your purpose and mission statement what is most known about you. Over time, you will be able to change features and develop products with new technologies that fulfil your mission.

Make sure your mission, and what you're bringing to the table is crystal clear. Could you tweet your mission? If you want to succeed at marketing, you should be able to summarize your offer in only one sentence.

I have researched the web and found the mission statement of some of the world's top brands. Try noticing the pattern:

- Instagram: "To capture and share the world's moments"
- CVS Pharmacies: "We will be the easiest pharmacy retailer for customers to use."
- Harley Davidson: "We fulfill dreams through the experience of motorcycling, by providing to motorcyclists and to the general public an expanding line of motorcycles and branded products and services in selected market segments."
- Microsoft: "At Microsoft, we work to help people and businesses throughout the world realize their full potential. "
- Nike: "To Bring Inspiration and innovation to every athlete in the world."
- Amazon: "To be Earth's most customer-centric company where people can find and discover anything they want to buy online."
- Google: "Google's mission is to organize the world's information and make it universally accessible and useful."

I've done the exercise myself to help you better understand the process. I call this example the "Mission Makeover". I invite you to have fun, and try it yourself! I've taken some random sample "feature statements," or basic "what I do" statements, and turned them into great brand missions.

We sell televisions. → We help generations see the world and live better experiences.

We write books for children to help them learn to read. → Our mission is to share meaningful stories with children and help them grow.

We create websites. → We connect brands to customers online.

We sell products for the kitchen and the house → The best memories happen in your home, and and we want to make those memories perfect through our products.

Remember to try to notice that great brand missions are timeless. For example, if tomorrow televisions don't exist, experiences and sights still exist. Try to focus on that.

If There is No Need, Convince People There is One

Let me introduce this concept to you by retelling a short story that took place in Europe, around 1900. The velvet industry was struggling. Experts were saying that it was impossible to make velvet fashionable; it was effectively dead. Industry leaders had no idea what to do.

Until they finally had a "Eureka!" moment.

They hired a persuasion expert and targeted two regions: Paris, and the United States.

First thing first, that person went to see top fashion designers and promoted velvet. He negotiated deals, partnerships and agreements for them to use velvet. After that, he went to see the most beautiful top models, and influenced them to wear velvet, especially the clothes created by the top designers.

Long story short, it was now trendy to use velvet in the fashion industry. Quickly, the journals were screaming: "Velvet is back! Velvet is back!" and the masses started wearing velvet more than ever; even becoming more popular than at its height.

Mission accomplished!

This is pure genius. They created a need, where there was none. They could have displayed a million ads per year promoting velvet, but it would have been wasted money. They could have distributed velvet to all the stores in the world, but that would have been wasted energy and space. Instead, they created a movement by using influencers all around the world.

This story tells us three things:

- Advertising can't create a need, influence does
- If you have no influence, use someone else's
- Don't market "stuff", market movements

If you are aware of the urban and pop world, you probably know about Cîroc. This vodka is nothing new. In fact, it is the same vodka as all the other ones in the liquor store shelves. So, how did it manage to grow from 50 000 bottles sold per year to more than two million in less than 6 years? Influencers.

Ok, of course there are other reasons, like having a quality product (their vodka is top quality), advertising consistency, strong distribution channels, and strong management skills, but mostly it is because of the influencers Diddy (Puff Daddy, Cîroc's co-owner) uses to market the brand. In fact, the day he started co-owning the brand, he started giving the spotlight to Cîroc by putting it in music videos, TV shows, high-end events, and photoshoots. It constantly found itself in the hands of influencing people. In no time, fans started telling themselves: If my idols are drinking Cîroc, I need to be drinking Cîroc. In fact, as humans, we copycat who we idolize.

The same thing happened with the clothing brand Fubu. Every year, top marketers and top brands use this concept to their advantage.

So, if your target market copycats who it idolizes, why not have them promote your brand?

One important lesson I was taught, as a child, was to say thank you. Regardless of the situation, big or small, to always say thank you when receiving a kind act from another individual. An extension of this knowledge was the idea that no matter how good, or bad, life can get, to always be thankful for it.

I first saw this as good parenting; my parents wanted me to be polite. Thank you's are far more than just politeness, however. It allows you to show the world that you appreciate what you receive, that you deserve it, and that you are someone that is worth spending time and resources on.

For me, it is now simplistically clear: the more I am thankful, the better I am treated by my environment.

Marketing Should be About Sustainability

This chapter is not just about growing your brand. This chapter is about something that encompasses everything we do: our world's economy. I think marketers play a major role in this mission, and that they should be proud of it. Marketers are the conductors of our consumption economy. People like to buy, and people need to buy. Marketers are there to keep this cycle going. We may not be able to change our methods of consumption; however, we can make sure we keep things as sustainable as possible.

I've asked myself before: how can we encourage this spending ideology, without encouraging environmentally damaging practices? This question has allowed me to truly understand the role of sustainability in marketing. Sustainability is a win-win: the environment remains healthy, and companies remain profitable. Recently, markets and consumers have become more and more sensitive to the environment, social responsibility, and overall economic health. To keep it simple, sustainable marketing is the science of blending marketing and environmentally-friendly practices to ensure a better future.

A great example of a brand that incorporates sustainability into their core ideologies is the UK food chain Pret-à-manger. They adopted a "no overnight selling" food policy. In fact, everything that has not been sold on the day it was made would be given to charitable organisations that deal with homeless people. Also, all their napkins are made of recycled fabric, and their drinks are only made with fruits or vegetables, nothing more. This type of approach has paid off for Pret-à-manger. In less than 2 years, their revenue grew from 377 million euros to 510 million. By being recognized for their impact on the world around them, they've seen increased client traffic. Clients know that buying from them benefits much more than just the owners.

Lately, to fight against homophobia, top brands like IKEA or Cheerios have started using homosexual couples in their advertising campaigns. As you know, brands have a great influence over the public, and using it to change the perception of how sexual orientation is viewed is an effective way to use that influence. Did you know that IKEA was the first to use homosexual couples in their ads in 1994? Marketing campaigns, such as this one, aid companies to change the world for the better, while giving their company morally upstanding image.

Another remarkable concept is with the clothing Tentree. For every product sold, they plant 10 trees. As I write this chapter, they have planted a total of 5 million trees. In 2012, they had only planted 105 000 trees. The more people heard of the good deed, the more they flocked to their business.

Toms, the shoemaker, did something very similar. Their campaign, "One for One", consists of giving away one pair of shoe to an impoverished child for every pair sold.

There are a lot more interesting examples that could inspire ideas on how sustainability can be integrated into marketing brands. I highly recommend you take a look at "sustainable marketing campaigns" for other ideas.

Seeing companies and brands donate some of their profits to charitable causes are always a welcome sight, for anyone. Hopefully, we see more of it in the future.

Whether it is for a complete line of products, a new brand, the entire organisation, or just for a specific marketing campaign, marketers can have an impact on our world. So my question is this: do you think your marketing campaign could change the world? Don't stop yourself; as the world brightens, so will your success.

Always Talk to the Decision Maker

When it comes to business development, selling, marketing or just making deals, one of the most important rules, if not the most important, is to talk and communicate to the right person. You might be the best salesman in the world, but that doesn't matter one second if you're talking to the wrong person; that person can't be closed.

The decision maker in Business-to-business selling

In business to business, talking to the right decision maker is critical. For example, if you try to sell a software that will improve the business' relationship with customers, pitching the sale to the Financial Director won't work. He might be a good start (I'll get to that later), but don't even think about closing him. It sounds simple and obvious, yet I've seen many entrepreneurs forget this concept. You can make him interested, but your goal is to get passed to the right decision maker. In this case, it would probably be the Marketing Director or the Communications Manager.

If you don't manage to contact the right decision maker directly, strive higher. Once you find a contact sitting high in the organization, ask to be referred to the right person. In fact, from my experience, it is much easier to be "pushed-down" in the organization than to be "pushed-up".

Don't be afraid to try to contact CEOs. In the last year, I've talked over the phone to a couple of Fortune 500 CEOs. They like audacity, and they see ambition when they receive an email. Don't be too pushy with your emails, try to stay cool. The first email should always be telling a story instead of selling.

The decision maker in Business-to-consumer selling

Who should you be ideally advertising to?

Let's take an example. Let's say that you are selling a new brand of men's boxers. Don't you wonder why ads for men's boxers frequently have an emphasis on sexuality? Why they're iconic, and usually provocative? Because they're advertised to women.

In fact, according to BusinessWeek magazine, Women spent 80% of all sport apparel dollars and controlled 60% of all money spent on men's clothing in 2013. The numbers aren't too different for underwear. This makes us realize that sometimes the decision maker is not who it appears to be at first glance.

Same thing for bank accounts, as women represent 89% of the decisions. For new houses purchases, 91%.

I am not saying that women decide everything we buy (that theory is for another time), I am saying that you should think twice about who really is your decision maker. It might be people completely outside your target market.

The same pattern is happening with kids. In fact, According to a study made last year by Nickelodeon, kids pick what to eat 85% of the time when visiting fast-food establishments. They also largely influence the purchasing decision for every meal of the week. And, I hope you know that kids watch television, making them very exposed to ads. So, brands started to put that to their advantage: they now make sure to market food to kids in a subtle manner.

I can already hear your thoughts: "But what do I do if my target market is not the same as the group I should be advertising to?" The answer resides in the content of your efforts and whom you will delight. But, the golden rule stays the same: influence the decision maker, sell to the target market. Take both into consideration, and treat every situation with care. Make sure you know who your target market is and who your decision maker is and strive to win both their hearts and loyalty.

So whether you are selling Business-to-business, or Business-to-consumer, it's imperative to talk to the right decision maker, the real one, or your efforts won't pay off.

Great marketers Know Nothing

As the famous saying by Michel Legrand goes: "The more I live, the more I learn. The more I learn, the more I realize, the less I know."

I believe this is quote is fits the world of marketers. I never said I know everything about marketing. In fact, I believe that no marketer does.

Read more books.

If you hate to read, or don't have time; make time.

Or, just read two pages a day.

Don't shy away from new things, new platforms, and new strategies. Jump on those opportunities as soon as you see them.

Nothing stays still; keep moving forward.

Follow your curiosity.

Meet new people.

Seek out knowledge at every turn.

Learn from mentors.

Take more courses. Not necessarily schooling; anything that can teach you something practical.

Be obsessed with research and new ideas.

Finally, understand we all know nothing.

Becoming a marketer/entrepreneur is an endless journey. The end goal, ironically, is to never reach a final destination.

"Marketing takes a day to learn. Unfortunately it takes a lifetime to master."
— Phil Kotler

This is the end

I hope you enjoyed going through this book, and learning lessons you can apply to your current and future projects. I invite you to follow me on my various networks, so that you may join me on my journey through the world of marketing.

- Instagram : @julesmarcoux
- Facebook : facebook.com/julesmrcoux
- Twitter : @julesmrcoux
- On my website : www.julesmarcoux.com

Also, I love receiving opinions on the content that I provide. I'll answer every email I receive. Shoot me an email at: jules@julesmarcoux.com

Thanks for taking part of this journey and sharing your love of marketing with me.

Finally, I want to thank all my clients that have trusted me since the beginning of my career. I am thankful for everything you've given me.

Cheers, to life!

Jules

Notes

Maggior, D. (2012, October 22). FedEx's Strategic Positioning Concept Absolutely, Positively Disrupted. Retrieved April 20, 2015, from http://www.innismaggiore.com/positionistview/read.aspx?id=104

Patel, N. (2013, June 27). What Converts Better: Free Trial or Money Back Guarantee? Retrieved April 30, 2015, from http://www.quicksprout.com/2013/06/27/what-converts-better-free-trial-versus-money-back-guarantee/

PressPausePlay Sneak Peek #1 - Seth Godin. (2011, February 22). Retrieved April 30, 2015, from https://www.youtube.com/watch?v=zXGAAvGoXMc

Company Facts. (n.d.). Retrieved May 2, 2015, from http://phx.corporate-ir.net/phoenix.zhtml?c=176060&p=irol-factSheet

Edwards, A. (2012, June 15). Mission Statements – World's Top 10 Brands. Retrieved May 2, 2015, from http://communicatingasiapacific.com/2012/06/15/mission-statements-worlds-top-10-brands/

MARKETING TO WOMEN QUICK FACTS. (2010, March 17). Retrieved May 5, 2015, from http://she-conomy.com/report/marketing-to-women-quick-facts

White, M. (2013, April 11). American Families Increasingly Let Kids Make Buying Decisions. Retrieved May 5, 2015, from http://business.time.com/2013/04/11/american-families-increasingly-let-kids-make-buying-decisions/

Gara, T. (2014, January 8). Can Diddy Repeat the Ciroc Magic With Tequila? Retrieved May 7, 2015, from http://blogs.wsj.com/corporate-intelligence/2014/01/08/can-diddy-repeat-the-ciroc-magic-with-tequila/

Bernays, E., & Miller, M. (2005). Propaganda. Brooklyn, N.Y.: Ig Pub.

Fournier, A. (2014, January 22). Une tirelire à 150 milliards de dollars pour Apple. Retrieved May 12, 2015, from http://www.lemonde.fr/technologies/article/2014/01/22/une-tirelire-a-150-milliards-de-dollars-pour-apple_4352477_651865.html

McNeilly, M. (2013, March 4). Price Promotions May Be Killing Your Brand: Here's What You Can Do About It. Retrieved May 12, 2015, from http://www.fastcompany.com/3006315/price-promotions-may-be-killing-your-brand-heres-what-you-can-do-about-it

Mourdoukoutas, P. (2013, September 27). A Strategic Mistake That Haunts JC Penney. Retrieved May 14, 2015, from http://www.forbes.com/sites/panosmourdoukoutas/2013/09/27/a-strategic-mistake-that-haunts-j-c-penney/

Lal, R. (2013, August 20). What went wrong at JC Penney? Retrieved May 21, 2015, from http://www.hbs.edu/news/articles/Pages/rajiv-lal-on-jcpenney.aspx

Buy a Bentley Continental Convertible ISR, Get a Breitling Limited Edition Chronograph for Free. (2011, November 29). Retrieved May 21, 2015, from http://www.carscoops.com/2011/11/buy-bentley-continental-convertible-isr.html

Fletcher, R. (2012, November 1). Ten Tree sees the forest and the trees. Retrieved June 23, 2015, from http://www.uregina.ca/business/assets/about-us/news/2012/Degrees-Ten-Tree-Winter2012.pdf

Shapiro, S. (2011, September 30). Why Business Plans Are Useless. Retrieved May 25, 2015, from https://www.americanexpress.com/us/small-business/openforum/articles/why-business-plans-are-useless/

Aloni, E. (2014, June 1). Plans are useless, but planning is indispensable. Retrieved May 24, 2015, from http://eran-aloni.com/2014/05/31/plans-are-useless-but-planning-is-indispensable/

Holt, D. (2015, April 23). Why long term marketing plans are worthless. Retrieved May 22, 2015, from https://inbound.co.uk/blog/why-long-term-marketing-plans-are-worthless/

Mankins, M. (2006). Stop Making Plans; Start Making Decisions. Retrieved May 23, 2015, from https://hbr.org/2006/01/stop-making-plans-start-making-decisions

Tjan, A. (2012, May 16). Great Businesses Don't Start With a Plan. Retrieved May 24, 2015, from https://hbr.org/2012/05/great-businesses-dont-start-wi/

Turnbull, A. (2015, January 22). Why This CEO Spends 20 Hours Per Week On Customer Support. Retrieved May 25, 2015, from https://www.groovehq.com/blog/startup-ceo-customer-service

Patel, S. (2014, December 21). How I Increased Conversion Rates By 250% By Talking To My Customers. Retrieved May 28, 2015, from http://sujanpatel.com/marketing/how-doing-customer-support-made-me-a-better-marketer/

Elliott, B. (2013, April 10). Seth Godin on Why Business Leaders Should Think Like Artists. Retrieved May 28, 2015, from http://www.entrepreneur.com/video/226328

Barros, M. (2013, July 9). Build Brand Awareness First - Distribution Second. Retrieved June 12, 2015, from http://marcbarros.com/build-brand-awareness-first-distribution-second/

Islam, M. (2011, August 8). Assignment on A case study of Red Bull Company. Retrieved June 23, 2015, from https://www.academia.edu/3696452/Assignment_on_A_case_study_of_Red_Bull_Company

Johnson, E. (2010, January 31). Brands to Last: Building a Winning and Enduring Brand. Retrieved June 23, 2015, from http://www.success.com/article/brands-to-last-building-a-winning-and-enduring-brand

10 Old Brands That Managed to Stay Modern. (n.d.). Retrieved June 23, 2015, from http://www.businessinsurance.org/10-old-brands-that-managed-to-stay-modern/

Buchanan, R. (n.d.). Examples of Firms Using a Push Strategy. Retrieved June 19, 2015, from http://smallbusiness.chron.com/examples-firms-using-push-strategy-14033.html

Berger, J. (2013). Contagious. London: Simon &
Schuster.

Fried, J., & Hansson, D. (2010). Rework. New
York: Crown Business.

Ries, A., & Trout, J. (1993). The 22 immutable
laws of marketing: Violate them at your own
risk. New York, NY: HarperBusiness.

28490889R00107

Made in the USA
Middletown, DE
17 January 2016